Second Edition

TEXAS Family Style

Second Edition

Great places to go to have fun with your kids

Contributing Authors

Cassie Bascope
Gail Drago
Frances Lowe
Carolyn Thompson
Meg Tynan
Ruth Wolverton

Coordinating Editor

Ann Ruff

Lone Star Books
A Division of Gulf Publishing Company
Houston, Texas

Texas Family Style

Second Edition

Library of Congress Cataloging-in-Publication Data

Texas—family style.

　First ed. authored by Ruth N. Wolverton.
　Includes index.
　1. Texas—Description and travel—1981—Guide-books.
2. Family recreation—Texas—Guide-books. I. Bascope,
Cassie. II. Wolverton, Ruth. Texas—family-style.
F384.3.T43　　1988　　　　917.64′0463　　　　87-35255
ISBN 0-88415-850-0

First Edition, July 1981
Second Edition, April 1988

CONTENTS

INTRODUCTION

Texas—Family Style/2nd Edition is more than just a guidebook to places to see in the Lone Star State that kids of all ages will enjoy. It's full of helpful hints to make travel with youngsters a real pleasure, not a chore. Written by parents who travel with their children, the book offers the best that Texas has to offer for family fun. Within these pages you'll find boat rides, train rides, parks, museums, wildlife refuges, and living history centers. You'll find ranches, caves and forts and a whole lot more places adults as well as kids will enjoy.

This second edition has been completely rewritten, providing the latest information on the well-known as well as the obscure attractions in the state. More than 200 places are described and the book has been organized to reflect how families travel. Instead of suggesting prearranged tours (which rarely fit your travel plans), the book tells about the sights found in each major city in one of four regions (see map). A map precedes each region pinpointing the towns with the outstanding attractions you won't want to miss. Towns are listed alphabetically within each region. Note that many of the attractions list a phone number and address so you can get further information and recheck the hours open.

So pack up the car, load up the kids, get out your roadmap, and open *Texas—Family Style* for a vacation your family will remember with pleasure.

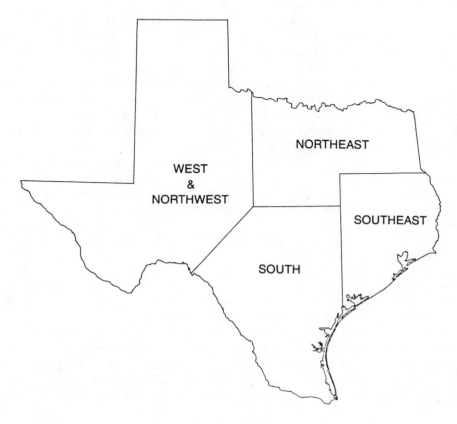

STARTING OUT

Even if you've pulled off the road, glared at your red-faced, sullen spouse and your tear-stained, jelly-smeared offspring noisily wallowing in the refuse heap that once was the backseat, and wailed, "I'll never go anywhere with you all again!"—read on. This was written especially for you and all the other parents out there who love travel but have children. We won't promise to transform you and yours into the smug couple with the immaculate kids of travel-poster fame, but we'll show you how to have a great time—with the kids—on your next weekend or vacation trip.

Honestly, traveling with kids can be fun, whether you have a tiny baby, an active toddler, a bubbling pre-schooler, or even a combination of the above, with a leery second grader thrown in for good measure. And no masochistic tendencies required, we guarantee. Look at it this way: If you want travel companions with fresh viewpoints, who thrive on new sights, sounds, and smells, who are willing to share any or all of your interests enthusiastically (at least for a few minutes), who are your most uncritical admirers and never bored with your company, you can't do better than your children. And all you need to do to cash in on this usually-hidden treasure is to make special provisions for special needs—yours and the kids.

That's what this book is all about.

Now assemble your family, hand everyone who can write a piece of paper, and ask them to record four things they most want to do on your trip. The younger ones can dictate their choices, and you will have to use educated guesses for those members of the family whose language development is in the ga-ga-goo-goo stage. Four is the magic number because it allows the fulfillment of the traditional three wishes and gives the adults an out when the eight-year-old requests hang-gliding, or the six-year-old requests marine exploration à la Cousteau. On the whole you'll find that you'll be able to grant everyone three wishes for each trip, no matter how divergent they seem in the beginning.

Once your list of wishes, your skeleton trip, is set, study this book. Share it with the family. You'll be surprised: Some of the items that you mention will bring excited oohs and aahs while others, for no discernible reason, will be greeted with bored yawns. Next, with the help of a good map, mark off a route which encompasses the wish lists and as many extra things as you'd like to include—and never mind the detours. Not yet.

At this point you may come to a shuddering halt as you total up the mileage and are hit by the grim fact that said mileage will be covered in complete togetherness with your young. This is also the point where most of the uninitiated panic and opt for still another "At Home" vacation. But you won't. You don't need to cop out anymore. Our Visitor-from-a-Small-Planet approach plus our great R & F innovation will take all the grimness out of that prolonged togetherness and is guaranteed to build in fun for all.

To use the Visitor-from-a-Small-Planet approach (also referred to as the VSPA), pretend that your kids have just arrived from Centurio III in the outer galaxy. The little aliens speak basic English and have acquired a sketchy knowledge of the quaint customs and strange sights so familiar to inhabitants of the Blue Planet. As good hosts you will, of course, tell your visitors in advance about the places they are going to see. You'll show them pictures and fill them in on some of the necessary background information. You won't take any pre-knowledge for granted. You'll describe the activities they'll engage in, explain exactly what they'll be doing when, and why it'll be such fun. You'll point out any required safety rules and give them the reasons for them. And, lastly, you'll gladly answer all questions and clear up any misconceptions which might lead to unnecessary fears and tensions.

During the actual excursions you'll stay close to your little aliens, remind them of your previous discussions about the places and activities, make sure that they understand what they see, point out details and associations they might miss, and, most importantly, share your own enthusiasm and enjoyment with them.

Finally, before you trundle your little aliens off to their home planet, spend some happy times with them reminiscing about your shared experiences. And that, friends, is a no-fail recipe for delightful sightseeing with your children anywhere and everywhere.

The Visitor-from-a-Small-Planet approach has a corollary: Every little alien needs a complete life-support system consisting of adequate living space, comfortable and neat garments, necessary equipment for easy care, and ample playthings for amusement. We've found travel in the family car the easiest way to provide these life-support systems most adequately and inexpensively.

To provide comfortable living space in a sedan for children up to five years or so, pack the leg room of the back seat with luggage so the child will have a level surface to play, sleep, and stand on her head. Furnish the place with the child's favorite blanket and pillow. If there are two children, the pillows and blankets delineate personal space. Blessed are those who are equipped with station wagons, for they cannot only assign more space per head, but set up a musical-chair sort of system so that each child has a different space each day.

To keep their living space, and yours, from resembling the morning-after-the-rock-concert in a few short hours, you'll need to post and enforce three rules: 1) no food or drink in the car other than water from the thermos and gum (you keep the wrappers); 2) no shoes (except adults, and all shoes are kept in front); and 3) only one toy per child at any one time. While they seem a bit arbitrary, the rules have been carefully developed over a long trial-and-error period. And, once you establish them, the rules are easy to enforce and really pay off.

As far as clothing is concerned, four outfits per person (except for your baby and/or toddler who'll need six) will do nicely. You'll wash every third day, so you'll have a margin of safety. A pair of extra shoes, swimsuit, pjs, and a sweater for each will round out the travel wardrobe. Use a separate bag—tote, flight, what have you—for each person if you can. It saves pawing through mountains of clothes to find that missing baby sock or size 3 bikini top.

Go long on equipment even if it tends to look as if you were about to begin your forty years in the desert. For baby take the stroller, the porta-crib or playpen, and the infant seat. Add a backpack if you plan to hike a lot. Incidentally, babies are super travelers. Their routine is easily managed en route: You are right there in the front seat, and if you have a bottle baby, the lighter on your dash will heat baby's bottle warmer. The motion of the car has a soothing effect on infants, and even sightseeing is a cinch if you tuck baby in his stroller and the rest of his life-support system in a diaper bag.

Toddlers need a stroller, the porta-crib or playpen (kids that age often get skittish about strange beds), and if you have one of those outdoor kiddie fences—

A restful stop beside cool water can do wonders for the moods of kids and adults alike.

that super deluxe floorless playpen bit—bring it along so your toddler can exercise safely while you do your thing. If you're training the child, be sure to tuck in the nursery chair or toilet seat.

Your two- to four-year-old will also appreciate her own toilet seat while traveling. Bring your stroller if the child still fits into it. Otherwise get one of those halter-leash arrangements. While some people object to it, we found it much nicer than dragging the child around by the hand, which, after a bit, gets quite uncomfortable and even painful for the child. If you think I'm exaggerating, try walking around with your arm held above your head for five whole minutes and you'll doubt me no more.

When it comes to toys, take along whatever the child currently enjoys. The only no-nos are musical or noise producing toys, which are nerve-wrecking in close quarters; anything sharp or potentially hurtful such as jacks, Yo-Yo's, and tinkertoys (you can bring them along in the trunk if your child insists and let him use them when not in motion); and playthings that have a trillion tiny pieces that get scattered all over. Jigsaw puzzles, however, are fine if worked inside a large cardboard box, and so are Legos because they stick together. Pack action toys—balls, jump ropes, Frisbies, and such—in the trunk. For the interior of the car you can use beer cartons, decorated or not, or large ice-cream cartons à la Baskin Robbins for toy boxes.

Now we come to the last of the famous trio, the R & Fs, short for Run and Fun stops. They are probably the most important item in the Travel Survival System. R & Fs provide a travel framework for regular meals, exercise, and rest. They are scheduled every hour and a half if there is a toddler aboard, every two to two and a half if the crew is pre-school and school age. R & Fs consist of fifteen minutes of vigorous activity, a nourishing snack or meal, depending on the time of day, plus the inevitable restroom routine.

This is how R & Fs work. At the specified intervals stop at a roadside or city park, chase the youngsters from the car and let them run for about five minutes or so. Then get out one of the special action toys from the trunk and use it, as President Kennedy used to say, ". . . with vigor." A few minutes of rope jumping is guaranteed to turn a hyper seven-year-old or a short-tempered spouse, for that matter, into a boon travel companion. Restroom stops are next on the agenda, followed by snacks. Serve small portions of protein foods: cheese, nuts, meats, seeds, raw vegetables, and something crunchy like bread sticks or pretzels, and small portions of non-drip fruit. For a drink try iced peppermint or cinnamon spice tea sweetened with a bit of honey. By the way, limiting the sugar intake on trips and otherwise often help your child's disposition quite a lot. Also, the snacks will keep the food intake on schedule and prevent any incipient motion sickness. After the snack (or meal if it happens to be that time of day), take a few minutes for a rousing game of tag or short distance races before you clean up the kids and load them back in the car. Total elapsed time: about 20 minutes. Benefits in relaxation and driving safety are tremendous.

If you like you can combine an R & F with a bout of sightseeing thusly: If you've been driving for more than an hour, let the children have their running bit, omit the toy playtime and proceed directly to the restroom. Give them their snack, clean them up, and then do your sight-seeing. If you walk a lot you can just load the kids in the car when it's time to move on. If, however, there was a lot of standing, sitting, or otherwise confined movement, take an additional five minutes and go through the tag or race routines before you distribute drinks, take them to the restroom, and continue your travel.

An R & F variation for bad weather, or when the urge for a hamburger and a fresh cup of coffee becomes too overwhelming, is as follows. Jog around the block with the kids before you enter the restaurant, and again before you get back in the car. In downpours, snowstorms, duststorms, and other natural or man-made interferences with the R & F routines, jumping jacks will save the day for you. They can be executed anywhere: in the restrooms, in halls, between tables, and in the aisles. If people stare, have one of your children announce in a clear voice, "We're the Blank family and we are in training." This, for some reason, seems to have the effect of transforming you instantly into a sort of Phys. Ed. Trapp Family, and people accept it without question.

You now have our complete Travel Survival System, which in conjunction with the book in your hands should make your traveling in Texas as delightful as ours has been.

Cassie Bascope
Gail Drago
Frances Lowe
Ann Ruff
Carolyn Thompson
Meg Tynan
Ruth Wolverton

Other great Lone Star Books packed with ideas for the traveling family:

Ray Miller's *Eyes of Texas® Travel Guides*:
Dallas/East Texas, 2nd Edition
Fort Worth/Brazos Valley
Hill Country/Permian Basin
Houston/Gulf Coast, 2nd Edition
Panhandle/Plains
San Antonio/Border, 2nd Edition
Ray Miller's *Houston*
Ray Miller's *Texas Forts*
Ray Miller's *Texas Parks*

The Alamo and Other Texas Missions to Remember
Amazing Texas Monuments and Museums
Backroads of Texas/2nd Edition
Beachcomber's Guide to Gulf Coast Marine Life/2nd Edition
The Best of Texas Festivals
Bicycling in Texas
Camper's Guide to Texas Parks, Lakes, and Forests/2nd Edition
Dutch Oven Cooking/2nd Edition
Frontier Forts of Texas
Great Hometown Restaurants of Texas
A Guide to Fishing in Texas
A Guide to Historic Texas Inns and Hotels/2nd Edition
A Guide to Texas Rivers and Streams
Hiking and Backpacking Trails of Texas/2nd Edition
Historic Homes of Texas
A Line on Texas
Mariner's Atlas: Texas Gulf Coast
Rock Hunting in Texas
Texas Birds: Where They Are and How to Find Them/2nd Edition
Traveling Texas Borders
Unsung Heroes of Texas
Why Stop? A Guide to Texas Historical Roadside Markers/2nd Edition

NORTHEAST

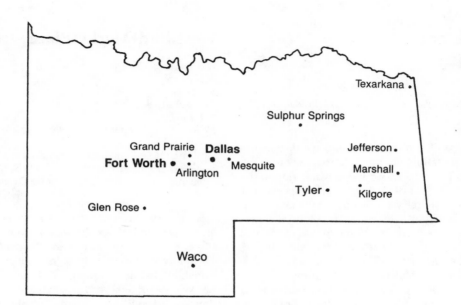

Texarkana

Sulphur Springs

Grand Prairie   **Dallas**   Jefferson

Fort Worth   Mesquite   Marshall

Arlington   Tyler   Kilgore

Glen Rose

Waco

Dallas

Reunion Tower

300 Reunion Blvd.
Dallas 75202
214-741-3663
Hours: 10 a.m.–midnight, Mon.–Fri., 9 a.m.–midnight, Sat.–Sun.
Admission charged.

In spite of its aura of sophistication and glamor, Dallas has a lot to offer for a family vacation. A unique way to begin a Dallas tour is to take a 68-second elevator ride to the top of Reunion Tower. Not only do you get a spectacular view of Dallas, you can get your bearings on downtown. The view from the lookout level is also fabulous at night, and kids will be delighted with the vast expanse of colorful city lights. You certainly won't have any trouble finding Reunion Tower. It's the 50-story shaft with the gigantic "Sputnik" ball on top, a very distinctive Dallas landmark.

Look to the northeast, and you'll see the reconstructed version of **John Neely Bryan's** log cabin at 600 Elm Street. The founder of Dallas sold his interest in his townsites for $7,000, which was a hefty sum in 1852. But, by 1877 Bryan was a hopeless lunatic and died in the state asylum. The cabin and terrazzo map indicating settlements in the county by 1846 are part of the **Dallas County Historical Plaza**.

Your kids may not be familiar with John F. Kennedy, but here is a good place to tell his tragic story. The **Kennedy Memorial** at 600 Main is directly across from the plaza. The controversial memorial by architect Philip Johnson represents a cenotaph, or empty tomb, and was funded by citizens of Dallas County in 1970. If you want your kids to know the details of Kennedy's assassination, the **Dallas County Administration Building**, formerly the Texas School Book Depository, is just north of the plaza at 411 Elm. This is the building where Lee Harvey Oswald fired the shots on November 22, 1963, that killed America's 35th president.

But, on a happier note, you are also at the beginning of Dallas' **West End Historical District** and the multitudinous attractions of the West End MarketPlace.

West End MarketPlace

West End Historical District
603 Munger
Suite 600
Dallas 75202
214-954-4350
Hours: 11 a.m.–10 p.m., Mon.–Thurs.; 11 a.m.–midnight, Fri.–Sat.; noon–8 p.m., Sun.
How to get there: Located on the north end of Market Street at Munger Avenue. The MarketPlace is at the west end of Woodall Rodgers Freeway, near the Arts District and the Dallas Convention Center.

For a very different kind of shopping and dining experience visit Dallas' 240,000-square-foot West End MarketPlace. Housed in what was the Brown Cracker and Candy Company in the early 1900s and later in the twenties the Sunshine Biscuit Company, this totally renovated structure has kept its original red brick exterior and interior walls. Today, the MarketPlace is a visual focal point against the Dallas skyline at night with its three water towers ringed in rainbow-colored neon. The heart of the building features an 85-foot-high skylit atrium complete with water fountains and eight 45-foot Alexander Palm trees. One of the original four ovens that were used during the Roaring Twenties to make candy, crackers, and cookies is still intact on the fourth floor.

But besides being a visual spectacle, the MarketPlace will delight visitors at the variety of unique stores and dining spots. One of the gift boutiques, for instance, caters strictly to dogs and cats with everything from designer jeans for canines to (if you can believe it) bridal outfits. Other one of a kinds include the Fudgery, where employees have been known to break out in song, a create-your-own-shoe store, and the Texana Bazaar where everything Texan from boots to buckles can be bought.

For an old-fashioned lunch, complete with chicken-fried steaks, mashed potatoes and thick milk shakes, try Bubbles Beach Diner, a 1940s rendition of the now extinct city diners. The children's menu offers all the kid favorites, so make this one a must.

Of course, if you want to eat fast, the International Food Bazaar with cuisines from all over the world is located on the fourth floor. Save some time to shop from some of the pushcarts resembling Conestoga wagons and manned by vendors in the area known as Bryan's Trading Post. There's always entertainment provided by roving jugglers, clowns, magicians, and musicians that is reminiscent of the old time market places.

Dallas Zoo

621 East Clarendon Drive
Dallas 75203
214-946-5155
Hours: 9 a.m.–6 p.m., daily, April–Sept., 9 a.m.–5 p.m., daily,
  Oct.–March.
Admission charged.
How to get there: Take I-35 South to the Ewing Ave. exit, then follow
  the signs.

Dallasites love their zoo, and great plans are underway for expansion in the near future. To really experience any zoo, a leisurely stroll is the only way. But, don't despair if your kids are small; strollers are available, and there are lots of benches and picnic tables for a rest. Also, concession stands offer the usual refreshment fare.

As the Dallas Zoo is one of the largest in Texas, you should plan on a full day to see it all. Also, time your visit to be at the primates' cages at 3 p.m. when they feed the gorillas and monkeys. Their incredibly funny antics will delight the audience.

One of the Southwest's best collections of antelopes is at the Dallas Zoo. These graceful creatures are marvelous to watch, even in captivity. Be sure to see the very rare and endangered okapi. It looks somewhat like a short-necked giraffe with a zebra rear end. Only about 20 of these unique creatures are in the U.S., and each costs approximately $250,000.

In the Children's Summer Zoo, kids can see, hear, and touch animals they only read about in the classroom. It is held from Memorial Day through mid-August.

Dallas Arboretum and Botanical Garden

8617 Garland Road
Dallas 75218
214-327-8263
Admission charged. (Children under six admitted free.)
Hours: 10 a.m.–6 p.m., Tues.–Sun., Mar.–Oct. 10 a.m.–5 p.m.,
  Tues.–Sun., Nov.–Feb. Closed Mondays, Christmas Day, and New
  Year's Day.

Within minutes of downtown Dallas where modern skyscrapers remind visitors that the city has come of age, the Dallas Arboretum and Botanical Garden adds serenity and natural beauty to the pressurized atmosphere of urban life. Sixty-six acres of rolling meadows and flowering gardens are adorned with an array of hues only God can create. The spring and summer are the best times to visit the arboretum because it's then that tulips, chrysanthemums, and daffodils color the green expanses of manicured grass.

If you find yourself in Dallas in the fall and at Christmas, call to find out when officials have scheduled their annual Fall Color Festival and the holiday Christmas at DeGolyer. The **DeGolyer House**, located on the grounds, is of special note here and is open for tours from 10 a.m. to 4 p.m. on operating days. This lovely estate, built for Mr. and Mrs. Everett L. DeGolyer in 1939, holds a prominent place on the National Register of Historic Places. The 1938 Camp Estate, now the headquarters for the Dallas Arboretum and Botanical Society, was designed as a focal point of a beautiful 22 acre estate by the famous Texas architect, John Staub, for Mr. and Mrs. Alex Camp.

With White Rock Lake as its background, the garden is a great place for an energy-charged child to expend a little energy.

Old City Park

1717 Gano
Dallas 75215
214-421-5141
Hours: 10 a.m.–4 p.m., Tues.–Fri., 1:30 p.m.–4:30 p.m., Sat.–Sun.,
  Closed Monday.
Admission charged.

Tucked away from the roar of cosmopolitan Dallas is a nostalgic return to the past at Old City Park. Kids are always fascinated with "how things used to be," and mom and dad couldn't ask for a better example of life at the turn-of-the-century than Old City Park. You can turn back the clock to 1840 and watch time pass until about 1910. The old dog-trot cabin starts your tour, and it ends with Victorian homes and a "shotgun" house. Rooms were built in a row, and if you fired a shotgun from the front door, the bullet would go right through the house and out the back door.

Social life centered around the church and general store, and a Sunday afternoon concert at the gazebo was where everyone went to see and be seen. Old City Park's gazebo still holds concerts and couples still get married in the old frame church. **McCall's Store** is a museum gift shop featuring items that might have been available in the 1800s. Don't miss the Central Texas fare served up at the **Brent Place Restaurant** (lunch only) in one of the restored homes. However, the kids will probably prefer popcorn and hot dogs from the 1900 Cretor's Popcorn Wagon. Tours are conducted by docents, and good behavior is expected from their small visitors, but a vast expanse of lawn offers plenty of space for running and playing.

Kids can easily understand how things used to be a long time ago at Dallas' Old City Park.

Olla Podrida

12215 Coit Road
Dallas 75251
214-934-3603
Admission free.
How to get there: Located between LBJ (635) Freeway and Forest Lane
* in Park Central.*

Olla Podrida, a unique shopping experience, is the answer to the dream of everyone who likes to shop. On the other hand, it could be a miser's nightmare because you could easily spend your life savings here in one afternoon. Still, meandering from shop to shop is well worth the time and indeed a cultural experience in itself.

For, Olla Podrida is the mutual meeting ground for area artists who allow wide-eyed children to observe them exercise skills that have made their works so desirable. Actually, creative energies are so strong here you leave wondering if it's too late to discover your own hidden talents. Everywhere you turn there are glass blowers, stained glass cutters, sculpturers, and leather artisans hard at work at their crafts.

Also under the center's steep wooden roof characterized by endless balconies, rafters, colorful banners, are unique shops that would delight even Scrooge himself. There are educational toy stores, novelty shops with musical carousels, carved circus figurines, and antique dolls. There is even a store full of tiny doll house canopy beds, armoires, kitchen sinks, and other furnishings.

You'll see everything here from military memorabilia to winemaking to Indian artifacts. Plan to stay for lunch. Olla Podrida has its share of kid food.

Fair Park

Friends of Fair Park
P.O. Box 26248
Dallas 75226
214-426-3400
Hours: Open year round
Admission free except during fair times in October.
How to get there: From U.S. 45 or Highway 75 (Central Expressway),
* take I-30 East to 2nd Avenue Exit. Fair Park lies straight ahead.*
* Parking available on grounds*

Dallas' Fair Park, open year round, is the home of the Cotton Bowl and the largest state fair in the United States. If you've never been to a state fair and if you find yourself in the vicinity of Dallas during the month of October, you shouldn't miss this very "Texas" event. The first sight to greet every visitor is ever-present Big Tex, a giant mechanical cowboy who welcomes everyone with a thunderous "Howdy!" Once you pass through the state fair portals, the teeming midway alive with rotating ferris wheels, bumper cars, merry-go-rounds, and barkers calling from their colorful carnival booths is sure to make even the oldest heart skip a happy beat. Of course, the scene takes on its own special magic at night when the midway lights up the Texas sky.

Once you tire of the carnival, venture into the exhibition halls where auctioneers speak their own language as they officiate livestock auctions, Future Farmers take pride in showing off their prize-winning calves, turkeys, and pigs, and ranchers compete with one another by bidding high prices for champion steers. Indeed the sights and sounds are all there, but the smells of Texas barbecue, corn-on-the-cob, and homemade bread will make you a slave to your surroundings.

So, to get a true "taste" of the Lone Star state, take your family to the State Fair of Texas. It's the best fun Texas has to offer!

The Fair Park Museums

In 1936, the State Fair of Texas celebrated the hundredth anniversary from Mexico. As a result, Dallas, the site of the Texas Centennial Exposition, became the concentration point for state pride and effort. Today, many of the buildings from this grand era still stand as a lasting memory to Texas' Centennial celebration. A blend of classicism, Art Deco, and traditional Texas motifs, the Centennial buildings, which are on the Register of Historic Places, house a variety of museums. The ones you choose to visit depend upon the interest level and the age of your children.

Whatever choices you make, you and your children will enjoy the well-kept grounds, and if all fails, there is the standby duck pond, complete with hungry ducks that love stale bread. So, be prepared by packing a lunch and duck food. This vast conglomerate of buildings houses six museums and a seventh, the African-American Museum, is scheduled to open soon. Other plans include the 30,000-square-foot Museum of Dallas, five acres of gardens and educational facility for the Garden Center and a 50-foot planetarium for Science Place.

The Science Place I
214-428-7200
Hours: 9:30 a.m.–5:30 p.m., Tues.–Sun.
Admission free.
How to get there: Located within Fair Park across from the Lagoon

If you have a future doctor in your midst, by all means, visit the Science Place. Everything you've ever wanted to know about the human body and then some is located in this hands-on museum. Health and medicine, physical and life sciences, machines and technology are the menu items here with emphasis on traveling exhibits. In the past, traveling exhibitions have varied from a presentation on China and its 7000-year-old history to riding on a flywheel car.

For more emphasis on space, visit Science Place II planetarium, also located in the park between M. L. King Blvd. and Pennsylvania Avenue on first Avenue.

The Dallas Aquarium
214-670-8441
Hours: 9 a.m.–5 p.m., Mon.–Sat., noon–5 p.m. Sun.
Admission free.
How to get there: Located on the fair grounds across from the band shell and amphitheater.

For our five-year-old, the Dallas Aquarium was a clear-cut winner among the Fair Park sites. Designed with kids in mind, the fish are very visible to those who still have years to grow. The facility is one of the largest inland aquariums in the United States and is the haven for 340 species of aquatic animals from all parts of the world, including a large collection of Texas fish. The most popular residents include a giant alligator gar, a school of piranhas, blind cave salamanders, and a 60-pound catfish.

The Dallas Museum of Natural History
214-670-8457
Hours: 9 a.m.–5 p.m., Mon.–Sat., noon–5 p.m. Sun.
Admission free.
How to get there: Located on fairgrounds across from the Lagoon off First and Grand Avenues.

Another favorite of children, particularly those who love dinosaurs, the Dallas Museum of Natural History tells the history of the state's environment and its native creatures. Fifty realistic dioramas depict birds, mammals, and plants native to Texas with other displays including a 75-million-year-old mammoth, an ice age mosasaur, and fossil seashells estimated at being a million years old.

The Dallas Civic Garden Center
Hours: 10 a.m.–5 p.m., Mon.–Sat., 12:30 p.m.–5 p.m. Sun.
Gardens open daily
Admission free.
How to get there: Located in Fair Park.

This lovely Garden Center, one of the oldest and largest civic gardens in the Southwest, features a 5,800 square-foot conservatory with tropical and sub-tropical plants from South America, Africa, and the Pacific Islands. The children will enjoy the miniature rose garden, and if you're a fan of Elizabethan literature, you'll appreciate the Shakespearean Garden. Also of interest is the herb and scent garden for the blind. Kids are allowed here to stop "and smell the roses." You'll also see some endangered species. I suggest, however, you keep little noses and fingers away from these.

The Age of Steam Railroad Museum
Hours: 9 a.m.–1 p.m. Thurs., Fri., 11 a.m.–5 p.m. Sat., Sun.
Admission charged.
How to get there: Located on Washington Street on the northern edge of Fair Park.

If you're a train buff or if your kids have never set foot on a train, travel on down to the Age of Steam Railroad Museum. A 1903 Dallas railroad station, the city's oldest, gives

Photo courtesy of Friends of Fair Park

Vintage trains at Dallas' Fair Park take visitors back to "old-time" Texas.

an air of authenticity to the museum that displays luxurious passenger cars, steam locomotives, sleepers, parlor-club cars, and diner cars. You can climb aboard for a stroll back in time.

The Texas Hall of State
214-421-5136
Hours: 9 a.m.–5 p.m., Mon.–Sat., 1 p.m.–5 p.m., Sun.
Admission free.
How to get there: Located next to the Cotton Bowl Stadium.

The Texas Hall of State was built to tell the story of Texas history for the 1936 Centennial Exposition. Maintained by the Dallas Historical Society since that time, the museum displays a large collection of historical documents about Dallas and the state.

One last note: Before you leave the Fair Park, walk over to the **Texas Promenade,** which was created in honor of the Sesquicentennial. To mark the 150th birthday of Texas, state residents, many of them famous, purchased commemorative bricks to create the Texas Promenade. The walkway runs through the heart of Fair Park, and many of the bricks hold such prominent names as Greer Garson, Roger Staubach, Tommy Tune, and Sandy Duncan.

Call or write for more information concerning annual events, park festivities and special exhibits featured at the Fair Park and its museums.

Six Flags Over Texas

P.O. Box 191
Arlington 76010
817-461-FLAG
Hours: Open 10 a.m. summers; closing times vary. Times vary during off season.
Admission charged.
How to get there: Located on I-30 between Dallas and Fort Worth.

Six Flags Over Texas, the state's most popular theme park with over 200 acres of exciting rides and shows, deserves two days of your well-earned vacation. Your thrill-seeking children will delight at the wealth of rides. You'll be impressed with the clean grounds that are dotted with gardens alive with blooming flowers of every color and variety. There is no large expanse of concrete that makes the Texas sun unbearable. Water fountains add a coolness to what could be a dry, hot environment.

Actually, Six Flags has everything from clean bathrooms and a host of fast food restaurants to a mini amusement park designed with little ones in mind called Looney Tunes. Hosted by such favorites as Bugs Bunny and Daffy Duck, small kids can climb nets, ride little cars and trains and see Porky Pig, Sylvester and Yosemite Sam perform their slapstick antics.

For the teenager, there's every ride imaginable guaranteed to scare the living daylights out of them. A favorite is the churning waters of the Roaring Rapids, a ride reminiscent of a raft trip down the raging Colorado River. And, if they or you are into freefall, try the Texas Cliffhanger, where gondolas drop from the top of a 128-foot tower. Wait until after you've ridden this one to eat.

As for roller coaster enthusiasts, well, the Runaway Mine Train is a must for you if you like having your head jerked and jostled up and down along 2,400 feet of tubular steel track. If, however, you like the more traditional coaster, try Judge Roy Scream.

More than any other theme park in Texas, there seems to be an emphasis on rides that result in riders getting wet. For example, this is the birthplace of the world's first Log Flume ride, and in 1987, Splashwater Falls, a spectacular waterfall ride, was introduced and well received. With this in mind, particularly if you have a small child who becomes a Mr. Hyde when he gets wet, be sure to bring an extra change of clothes. If you decide to leave the park and return in the same day, be sure to get your parking ticket and your hand stamped to avoid paying an extra admission charge. And, if you plan to spend two days at Six Flags, buy a two-day pass. You'll save a little money this way.

Oh, and bring hats, suntan lotion, strollers, and by all means, wear tennis shoes. The concrete can roast sandled feet.

Fielder Museum

1616 West Abram
Arlington 76012
817-460-4001
Hours: 9:30–4 Tues. through Fri., 1:30–4:30 Sun.
Admission free.
How to get there: Take the Fielder Road exit from I-30 and go south on Fielder over the Highway 80 overpass. Turn left.

Originally the 1914 home of James Park Fielder, the Fielder Museum now resides in this residence that was one of the first brick homes in Arlington. Surrounded by beautiful old oak trees, this "house on the hill" overlooks the Fielder's 215-acre farm that was full of fruit orchards and vegetable gardens.

Today, the home provides the setting for visitors to learn not only about Arlington's past but also about community life as it existed at the beginning of this century. The museum has four permanent exhibits—the general store, and a turn-of-the-century barbershop, a bedroom scene, decorated with antique dolls, and the J. W. Dunlop photographic display of early Arlington. Temporary exhibits are

Photo courtesy of Six Flags Over Texas

Screaming, giggly riders add sound effects to the exciting Judge Roy Scream, the traditional wooden roller coaster at Six Flags Over Texas.

frequently displayed at the Fielder Museum with special emphasis on local artists and writers.

The Wax Museum of the Southwest

601 E. Safari Pkwy.
Grand Prairie 75050
214-263-2391
Hours: Open daily at 10 a.m. except New Year's Day, Thanksgiving, and Christmas; Closing hours vary.
Admission charged (children to age 3 allowed in free.)
How to get there: Located north off I-30, near Belt Line Road and five minutes east of Six Flags.

If you've never taken your family to a wax museum, you're in for a real treat. Actually "trick or treat" may be more appropriate as the entire experience leaves visitors with an eerie feeling that it is they who are being watched. The museum is inhabited by such idols as Clark Gable, Carol Lombard, John Wayne, Paul Newman, and Robert Redford, and only their frozen stances remind you that they're only wax. All of the Texas outlaws are here too, many with a noose around their neck.

You walk through one viewing room only to find yourself transported into another era characterized by authentic scenery and figures who made lasting names for themselves. Everyone is present from Jesus surrounded by his disciples to Will Rogers practicing his familiar rope tricks. All the most important events in American history are represented by characters who seem on the verge of speaking your name. Though they won't realize it, your kids will get a history lesson they'll probably never forget.

A word of warning, however, if you have children who have nightmares and who scare easily, have them skip Dr. Blood's Theatre of Horrors. Werewolves, vampires, mummies and ghosts inhabit this darkened corridor which has trick doors leading to monsters and goblins.

Also, the museum is designed as a kind of maze that connects viewing arenas. Many branch out to two and three scenes, and so it is very easy to get lost or be separated.

International Wildlife Park

I-30 and Belt Line
Grand Prarie 75052
214-263-2205
Admission charged.
How to get there: Take Belt Line exit off I-30, about half-way between Dallas and Fort Worth.

Of all the places to go with kids where a camera is an absolute must, it's International Wildlife Park. The elephant ride and the pony ride are each guaranteed to thrill kids and provide a perfect snapshot.

Allow a lot of time at International Wildlife Park because it takes the better part of a day to enjoy it all. Maybe it's best

to start with the six-and-a-half-mile drive through the park and see nearly 2,000 exotic animals from all over the world roam free. Get a bucket of animal food, in fact, two or three buckets would be wise. Nearly all of these critters are adept panhandlers and stand firmly implanted in the middle of the road and refuse to budge until they get their goodies. Little hands will just love the close contact with feeding the animals. Just be sure you don't give them people food. You can't get out of your car under any circumstances, but don't be surprised if a big elk nose comes poking through the window of your car demanding his handout. Curious ostriches come prancing by, and a placid camel ambles up for a taste of the free treats. Hey, make that four buckets of animal food.

After slowly driving through the park, catch the Wildlife Express as it chugs back paths of the park. Then, an absolute must is the **Best Little Circus in Texas.** Kangaroos box, chimpanzees race, a bear plays basketball, and gorgeous Macaw parrots put on a brilliant show, with their clever tricks.

Traders Village

2602 Mayfield Road
Grand Prairie 75051
214-647-2331
Hours: 8 a.m. to dusk Saturday and Sunday, year-round.
Admission free (except for parking fee).

Billed as the "Famous Texas Flea Market," Traders Village is for you if you love trash and treasures. More than 1,600 dealers congregate here to sell their wares that range from lamps to licorice. For acres, vendors and treasure hunters bargain to get the best from their dollar while the kids entertain themselves at the arcade, ride the antique merry-go-round, or watch the action in the rodeo arena. The market has become so popular, promoters have even created an RV park which is the largest of its kind in the Dallas/Fort Worth area. Go early or late, take a thermos, wear comfortable shoes, and hold on to your kids. If they get lost, you may never find them!

Samuell Farm

Rt. 4, Box 1274
Mesquite
512-285-4670
Hours: 9:00 a.m. to 30 minutes before sunset, daily.
Admission charged. No smoking and no pets allowed.
How to get there: East from downtown Dallas on I-20 and the Beltline service road.

The good old days of going to spend a summer with grandma and grandpa on the farm are a thing of the past. Grandma and grandpa live in a retirement resort and play golf instead of milking cows. However, some of the old-fashioned virtues of hard work on a farm still enchant kids at Samuell Farm, practically in the heart of Dallas.

Opened in 1982, this 340-acre farm is maintained just as though country life had never changed from the late 1800s. Chickens scratch in the dirt, old Dobbin pulls his wagon, a windmill pumps water, and best of all children can learn to quilt and make candles.

Mom and dad can set up camp and sign up for a family hayride or bait the hooks to dip in one of the seven fishing ponds. Samuell Farm's scenic trails are perfect for riding your horse, bicycling, or jogging.

Samuell Farms offers special events all year (even sausage stuffing) for kids, and a wonderful country store stocked with handmade crafts, toys and other general merchandise kids and grownups can't resist.

Fort Worth

Fort Worth Convention and Visitors Bureau

Dept. FPK
Water Gardens Place
100 E. 15th St., Suite 400
Fort Worth 76102
1-800-433-5747

Fort Worth, known to Texans as "Cowtown," has a rough and dusty history characterized by a people strong-willed and well-versed in the struggles of the early west.

It's true that Fort Worth is the home of the **Southwestern Exposition Livestock Show and Rodeo,** the historic stockyards, and **Billy Bob's,** the world's largest honky-tonk. However, the presitigious **Van Cliburn International Piano**

Competition also takes place here, and Fort Worth prides itself in its museum district that is composed of four world-class museums.

Also don't forget to stop by the **Fort Worth Water Gardens** downtown for a relaxing and refreshing break.

The Historic Stockyards District

How to get there: Traveling north or south on I-35 West, take the N.E. 28th Exit 54-A or B West to North Main Street, and turn South.

Over 10 million head of cattle were driven through the middle of Fort Worth on what is now Commerce Street. By

Cattle auctions take place weekly at the Livestock Exchange Building, located in the Fort Worth Stockyards.

Photo courtesy of the Fort Worth Convention and Visitors Bureau

1873, railroad lines linked Fort Worth to the stockyards where cattle waited to be taken to Kansas packing plants.

Visitors can visit the Fort Worth Stockyards, watch cattle auctions each week at the Livestock Exchange Building, eat a steak at the Cattleman's Steak House, see a rodeo at Cowtown Coliseum, and witness gunfights in Rodeo Plaza. They can take a stroll down Exchange Avenue, a haven for craftsmen who have learned the old ways to create chaps, saddles, boots and lassos. Local cowboys still frequent the saloons within the Stockyards including the White Elephant Saloon, where cowboy songs add to the authentic western atmosphere.

For more information regarding sights at the Historic Fort Worth Stockyards, contact the Fort Worth Convention and Visitors Bureau, Dept. FPK, Water Gardens Place, 100 E. 15th St., Suite 400, Fort Worth, Texas 76102, or call 1-800-433-5747.

The Fort Worth Museum District

Though Fort Worth is lovingly referred to as "Cowtown," it does have its share of cultural attractions. In fact, just west of downtown, visitors can ponder some of the most priceless art in the nation. Here in the Museum district are four museums ranked with the best art museums in the world. Located within walking distance of each other, the museums offer the touring family a chance to expand their cultural horizons. If, however, you feel the kids would be better off expending a little energy at the Fort Worth Zoo or going for a swim in the hotel pool, then by all means, head in that direction. If you have children that can be more subtly entertained, go to at least one museum.

The Amon Carter Museum

3501 Camp Bowie Boulevard
For Worth 76102
817-738-1933
Hours: 10 a.m.–5 p.m., Tues.–Sat., 1 p.m.–5:30 p.m. Sun. Tours
    daily at 2 p.m.
Admission free.
How to get there: Located at the corner of Montgomery Street and
    Camp Bowie Boulevard.

The collection here was assembled by the late Amon G. Carter, Sr., the Fort Worth publisher and philanthropist. This impressive museum houses paintings that represent American art from the past 150 years, including nineteenth-century landscapes by Thomas Cole and Winslow Homer and abstracts by Georgia O'Keeffe and Stuart Davar. Also included is a major collection by Frederic Remington and Charles M. Russell.

The Kimbell Art Museum

3333 Camp Bowie Boulevard
Fort Worth 76102
817-332-8451
Admission free.
Hours: 10 a.m.–5 p.m., Tues.–Sat., 11 a.m.–5 p.m., Sun.
How to get there: Located at Camp Bowie Boulevard and Arch Adams
    Street.

Considered one of the most outstanding art museums in the United States, the Kimbell Art Museum includes paintings by Duccio, Holbein, El Greco, Rembrandt, Cezanne, and Picasso. The museum also has collections of Egyptian, Greek, Pre-Colombian, African, and Asian art.

The Sid Richardson Collection of Western Art

309 Main Street
Fort Worth 76102
817-332-6554
Admission free.
How to get there: From the Cultural (museum) District, take Camp
    Bowie Boulevard to 7th Street. Follow 7th Street to downtown Fort
    Worth.

The Sid Richardson collection is composed of fifty-two American West paintings by Frederic Remington and Charles M. Russell. Most were collected by oilman and philanthropist Sid W. Richardson from 1942 until his death in 1959.

The Fort Worth Museum of Science and History

1501 Montgomery Street
Fort Worth 76102
817-732-1631

The Fort Worth Museum of Science and History will probably be the favorite among the kids. The museum features exhibits on Texas history, fossils, and geology, the human body and the history of medicine, and the world of the computer. And, yes, they do have dinosaur bones. Astronomy and laser light shows in the Noble Planetarium and exciting film presentations are shown in the Omni Theatre on a regular basis on an 80-foot diameter, domed screen that envelops you with sight and sound.

The Fort Worth Art Museum

1309 Montgomery Street at Camp Bowie Boulevard
Fort Worth 76102
817-738-9215
Hours: 10 a.m.–5 p.m. Tues.–Sat.; 10 a.m.–9 p.m., Tues. Sept.–July;
* 1 p.m.–5 p.m. Sun.*
How to get there: Located at Montgomery Street and Crestline Road.

The Fort Worth Art Museum displays twentieth-century paintings, sculpture, drawings, and prints. Such notables as Picasso, Rothko, Stella, Still, and Gottlieb are represented. Call or write the curator for information on frequent exhibitions, children's classes, lectures, film series and tours.

Japanese Garden

3220 Botanic Garden Drive
Fort Worth 76107
817-870-7686
Hours: 10 a.m.–5 p.m., Tues.–Sun. Closed Monday.
Admission charged.

You can visit Japan and not even leave Fort Worth. At the Japanese Garden, it is just like being in a serene garden in the Orient. Kids will absolutely love this enchanting "Gate of Heaven," for a Japanese garden is so different from those formal European gardens. Trees, plants, stones, rocks, sand, gravel and water all take on a special significance due to the Buddhist search for the feeling of *yugen*, or tranquility.

Of course there is a tea house, and the children will be fascinated by the Imperial Koi, the enormous carp that swim in the pool below. Believe it or not, some Koi sell for thousands of dollars. Feel free to feed these exquisite beggars, and remember that years ago, only royalty could possess these special fish.

In Japan, a moon-viewing deck is a large, flat-topped mound of clay. Here, the deck is made of concrete, and kids love to play on it when it isn't covered with spectacular floral arrangements.

It is so restful to stroll slowly through the Japanese Garden with its pagodas and shrines, and even the most rambunctious kids will feel the peace this lovely place creates.

You also won't want to miss Fort Worth's **Botanic Garden,** a 114-acre wonderland of beauty. Many programs are

Photo courtesy of Tourism Division, Texas Department of Commerce

Fort Worth's Japanese Gardens provide an Oriental flavor to Texas' Cowtown.

offered for children to teach them the beauty and importance of plants in our lives.

Fort Worth Zoo

2727 Zoological Drive
Fort Worth 76110
817-870-7050
Admission charged.
How to get there: Located one mile south of I-30 on University Drive.

A zoo is a fantastic learning place for kids. At the Fort Worth Zoo, the emphasis is on teaching the public, particularly the young, about the important role animals and their preservation play in our world.

Fort Worth has one of the best zoos in the Southwest, and its employees and docents work hard to keep it that way. One very special feature for kids are large wooden carts topped by brightly striped canopies and manned by docents. Kids can find anything from an ostrich egg to antlers, and every item is meant to be touched and held. Two mottos prevail: "Please Touch," and "Ask Me." Also very popular are the zoo's summer classes for children 6 through 16. On special "Keeper Days" kids can even follow zookeepers on their rounds and find out just what it's like to hand raise a baby orangutan or feed a python.

Pate Museum of Transportation

U.S. Highway 377
(Between Fort Worth and Cresson)
817-396-4305
Hours: 9 a.m.–5 p.m., daily. Closed Monday
Admission free.

Just a few miles south of Fort Worth is one of the best museums of transportation in Texas, and it's all free. Here is a great outing for the family, so bring a picnic and plan to spend the day.

Begin with a tour of the private railroad car the "Sunshine Special's Ellsmere." This classic example of Victorian elegance was built in 1914 for the president of the Wagner Palace Car Company. Later it was acquired by T&P Railroad and used as a president's car. Here is the last word in private railroad car luxury.

Next, go inside the huge barn-like building and see beautiful restorations of rare antique cars. Among all those grand old cars is a 1963 Checker Cab—it is the cab Lee Harvey Oswald took after the assassination of J. F. Kennedy.

Out on the museum grounds is an impressive array of army, navy and air force planes, tanks, and boats that kids can climb around on. Exhibits range from helicopters to transports to jet fighters. The Pate Museum is one of the very few museums to display a sea-going vessel inland. It is a Minesweeper Boat 5 and acquired through the U.S. Navy.

Glen Rose

Dinosaur Valley State Park

Box 396
Glen Rose 76043
817-897-4588
Hours: 8 a.m.–10 p.m., daily.
Admission charged.
How to get there: Located 4 miles west of Glen Rose on FM 201.

Kids are *always* fascinated with dinosaurs, probably because they were so big, and it seems incredible that the earth was really inhabited by such large ugly creatures—not a beauty in the bunch.

About 135 million years ago, give or take a few million, Texas was a vast swampy mushy place with lots of thick plastic mud ideal for creating fossils. Roaming around in this steamy swampland were the "terrible lizards." We know they were here, because they left their footprints behind in the oozy mud of the Paluxy River. You can see these birdbath-size footprints at Dinosaur Valley State Park, and the best time for viewing is in late summer when the river is very low.

Greeting you at the park are life-size replicas of a brontosaurus and a tyrannosaurus rex. Brontosaurus, or old "thunder lizard," weighed 40,000 pounds and one pound of that mass of reptile was his brain. As for tyrannosaurus rex, the big bugger walked upright with tiny front feet and had a mouthful of ferocious teeth. Both critters were made for the 1964 World's Fair and a gift of Sinclair Oil Company. The tracks at the park were made by neither of these beasts, but by a smaller sauropod.

Fossil Rim Ranch

Rt 1 Box 210
Glen Rose 76043
817-897-4967
Hours: 10:00 until one hour before sunset, Mon.–Fri., 9:00 until one
*   hour before sunset, Sat.–Sun.*
Admission charged.
How to get there: Located 3 miles west of Glen Rose off U.S. 67.

One of the most beautiful wildlife parks in Texas is Fossil Rim Ranch. You could swear you were in the heart of the African Veldt. The trees and grass aren't the same, of course, but there are all the animals that you travel thousands of miles to photograph in Africa right here in Texas.

Giraffes lope about, ostriches peck at your car window demanding their handout, and the endangered addax, oryx, and Grevy's zebra all find a welcome home here at Fossil Rim. A very special treat at this unique ranch is a visit to the cheetahs in their separate enclave. It's not possible to see them reach their top speed of 70 miles per hour in captivity, but you will love watching these magnificent streamlined cats play. Fossil Rim takes justifiable pride in its 17 cheetahs, one of the largest groups outside Africa.

The drive through is really spectacular, and you are provided a list of the animals on the ranch, their physical characteristics, and whether or not they are on the endangered list. At the **Overlook** restaurant, take a break and munch a hamburger or hot dog, and enjoy the gorgeous view from the rim of the ranch at the animals placidly grazing below.

Plan to spend the night at the charming **Inn on the River** in Glen Rose. This was once a sanitarium that is now one of the loveliest country inns in Texas (817-897-2101).

Texarkana

Texarkana Chamber of Commerce
816 State Line Avenue
Texarkana, USA 75501

Texarkana has a new museum to Scott Joplin that honors the great black musician known as "The King of Ragtime."

But, Joplin was eons ago in "kid-time," and they might be bored with the life of someone other than a rock star. However, they will get a kick out of a town where the state line runs right down its main street. Go to the post office and pose at the photographer's island with one foot in Arkansas and the other in Texas. Then, go over to Bryce's Cafeteria, an East Texas institution for good cooking.

Tyler

East Texas Chamber of Commerce
P.O. Box 1592
Longview 75606
1-800-262-8747

The famous **Rose Garden** (214-592-1661) open free to the public is here. While flowers may not be a high priority spot on a kid's idea of a fun vacation, take them to the Rose Garden anyway. It is a real treat to see 38,000 rosebushes with 385 varieties of America's favorite flower. And what is also so wonderful about the Rose Garden other than its beautiful landscaping is the sweet fragrance that lingers in the air from all of the roses.

Don't miss the **Caldwell Zoo** (214-593-0121). It's small by Texas standards, but absolutely wonderful. This gift of love to Tyler by Mr. and Mrs. D. K. Caldwell promotes concern through education for the survival of the animal kingdom.

Waco

Texas Ranger Museum

Fort Fisher Park
P.O. Box 1370
Waco 76703
817-754-1433
Hours: 9 a.m.–5 p.m., daily
Admission charged.

Tales of the Texas Rangers are the stuff of Hollywood westerns, but they are better than movies, for the Rangers actually lived those harrowing experiences. Their heroic feats are sure to impress any age group, and even everyone will enjoy the exhibits at the Texas Ranger Museum. The terrific gun collection houses rare pieces from famous outlaws and lawmen, such as Billy the Kid's Whitney shotgun and the Colt pistol that captured Geronimo. Also on exhibition is a tribute to the most famous Ranger of them all—The Lone Ranger.

Armstrong Browning Library

Baylor University
Waco 76706
817-753-3556
Hours: 9 a.m.–noon, 2 p.m.–4 p.m., Mon.–Fri., 9 a.m.–noon, Sat.
Admission free.

If your kids love literature, take them to the Browning Library at Baylor University. Even if they are too young for "How Do I Love Thee?" they will certainly know the story of the Pied Piper of Hamlin, even though they don't know the author was Robert Browning. This library was begun by a great teacher, A. J. Armstrong, who had local children act out this famous poem. The library is Armstrong's labor of love for the Brownings and many of their possessions are beautifully displayed.

Central Texas Zoo

P.O. Box 7344
Waco 76710
817-752-0363
Hours: 9 a.m.–5 p.m., Mon.–Fri., 9 a.m.–6 p.m., Sat.–Sun.
Admission charged.
How to get there: Take Lake Brazos Drive west off I-35. Follow signs to zoo.

The Central Texas Zoo is just plain fun! Their philosophy is a day at the zoo is a day with your family. Even though it's fairly small, here is a fine zoo that kids will love. Snakes seem to fascinate kids, and here are all the snakes indigenous to Central Texas. You might point out that the Braz Walker Aquarium was dedicated to an avid aquarium enthusiast who was struck by polio at 18, yet went on to write seven books and numerous scientific papers on tropical fish.

Folks at the Central Texas Zoo are justly proud of the fact that they were the first Texas zoo to successfully breed and hatch a bald eaglet in captivity as well as Bengal tigers, mountain lions, African leopards and other endangered species. Kids will enjoy King, the Bengal tiger as he splashes in his pond, and Max, the puma, who wandered into a garage in Carlsbad and ended up in Waco.

Texas Safari

Route 2
Clifton 76634
817-675-3658
Admission charged.
How to get there: From Waco, take State Highway 6 west to Clifton and follow the signs.

Where else would the "World's Largest Exotic Animal Drive-Thru Wildlife Park" be but in Texas? And, you definitely want your family to see this fantastic collection of animals from many parts of the globe. Five exciting sections make up Texas Safari. On the International Plains, 40 different species share the grasslands. At the Mount Kilimanjaro Preserve, the scenery becomes more breathtaking and the animals less apparent. Sharp eyes are needed, or you can rent binoculars if you forgot your own. The Texas Plains support the animals native to Texas such as white tail deer, elk, buffalo, mules, and wild turkeys. On The Ponds are birds of all kinds including the park's rare black-necked swans.

At the Trail's End, Safari Camp offers refreshments and many more animals to enjoy. The dangerous animals are in cages, as it would hardly do to let cats roam free in a park. And, kids will love the petting zoo with its animals that children can get to know. Best of all, there's also a nursery for baby animals.

Not only is the scenery and landscaping marvelous, but the whole park is so well planned, you will never forget your visit.

Brazos Queen II

Brazos River
817-757-2332
Hours: Restaurant: 5 p.m.–10 p.m., Sat., 11 a.m.–2:30 p.m., Sunday
brunch.
Public excursions: 3 p.m.–5 p.m., Sun. only, summer.
How to get there: From the Visitor's Bureau, turn under I-35 and just
after passing under I-35, turn right into the parking lot.

When you board the *Brazos Queen II* paddlewheeler, you step into Victorian elegance. The main dining room is beautifully decorated with a molded coffered ceiling, an enormous chandelier, handsome woodwork, and oriental carpeting. The cuisine is the best of early Texas and the Old South. Kids will be on their good behavior in this fine restaurant. If you are on board for the excursion, you will paddle along the historic waterways of the Brazos for a view of the Suspension Bridge, Lover's Leap, and other points of interest.

Waco Suspension Bridge

Indian Spring Park
University Parks Dr. across from Hilton Hotel

In 1866 there was not a single bridge across Texas' longest river, the Brazos. Money was scarce, and there were no facilities, equipment, or railroads to solve the problem. But, Texans were determined the Brazos needed a bridge. This 474-foot suspension bridge was completed in 1870 for the bargain-basement price of $135,000. Bricks and masonry were of local origin, while the cables and other steel work were provided by the firm of John A. Roebling & Son of New York, who later won fame as the builders of the Brooklyn Bridge. Still open to foot traffic and the symbol of Waco, the bridge's motto is "First Across and Still Across."

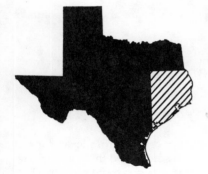

SOUTHEAST

Rusk

Lufkin

Woodville

Livingston

Romayor

Orange

Brenham   Spring   Beaumont

Sabine
Pass   Port Arthur

Houston

Brookshire   LaPorte
Seabrook

Alvin

Galveston

Alvin

Bayou Wildlife Ranch

P.O. Box 808, Route 5
Alvin 77511
Hours: 10 a.m.–6:30 p.m., May through Sept.; 10 a.m.–4 p.m., Oct.
through April; Open holidays. Closed Mondays October through
April.
Admission charged.
How to get there: Take Interstate 45 toward Galveston. At Dickinson,
take a right on FM 517 and go 6 miles. Located on FM 517 between
Dickinson and Alvin.

About a 45-minute drive from downtown Houston, the Bayou Wildlife Ranch ranks among the best wildlife preserves in its class. This 85-acre natural habitat, the pride of owner Clint Wolston and his wife, Barbara, is the home of 170 exotic animals, ranging from the Chapman zebra to the Watusi bull, a species that has survived over 7,000 years, to a giraffe named Ralph Sampson.

What makes the open-air tram trip around the ranch so enjoyable is the running commentary Clint gives about each animal as well as the flock of ostriches in constant pursuit of the tram full of tourists and their buckets of food. Yes, you can feed the animals, who are very happy to see you.

You'll learn facts such as one ostrich egg will fill four cups and camels store water, not in their humps or stomachs but in the tissues of their bodies. You'll see alligators, black swans, and Gertrude, the shaggy Scottish Highlander cow, and once your tour is complete, the kids can pet Duke, the ranch Great Dane.

Either before or after the tour, take a little time to go into the barn which is full of antique carriages. Ralph, the giraffe, is usually there to get away from the heat, along with an emu, and a couple of Thanksgiving-size turkeys, all very friendly.

Beaumont

Down south toward the coastline, you'll find the Golden Triangle, the Port Arthur, Beaumont, Orange complex, bordered on one side by the Sabine River and Lake, which empties into the Gulf of Mexico, and on the other, the Big Thicket. It's here that the land and the sea have provided for its people the rich natural resources of water, oil, timber, and rice-producing farmland as well as an area known as the "sportsman's paradise."

The Big Thicket National Preserve

National Park Service
3785 Milam
Beaumont 77701
409-839-2691

Photo by Michael Murphy. Courtesy of Tourism Division, Texas Department of Commerce.

The Big Thicket, described as the biological crossroads of North America, comprises 300,000 acres of Texas wilderness.

Big Thicket Museum

Big Thicket Association
P.O. Box 198
F.M. Highway 770
Saratoga 77585
409-274-5000

The Big Thicket, described as "the biological crossroads of North America," has within its 300,000 acres, a unique coexistence of seemingly incompatible life forms. Venture into this partially protected wilderness, and you'll see effects of the Ice Age, when glaciers far to the north pushed new species of plants and animals here that continued to thrive when the glaciers retreated.

Today biologists thrill at seeing the eastern hardwood forest existing with the arid southwestern desert, southeastern swamps, and central prairies. Bird lovers can capture with their lenses Eastern bluebirds nesting near roadrunners, and plant lovers can marvel at the prickly pear cactus co-existing with palmetto palms. Everywhere there is contradiction, yet balance.

If you decide to venture into this wilderness, 84,000 acres of which has been protected since 1974 by the National Park Service, do some research and planning first. The first thing you need to know is that the Thicket roughly goes from Livingston to Beaumont to Jasper.

Start by contacting the Big Thicket National Preserve office in Beaumont or the Big Thicket Association, a private group headquartered at the Big Thicket Museum in Saratoga. Both groups have much to offer; however, Park services are free of charge. They'll send you information on hiking trails, canoe trips, primitive camping sites, as well as pertinent information on the Big Thicket. They also offer guided hikes and canoe trips as well as informative seminars on local wildlife, flora, and Big Thicket folklore. There's even a class designed for children called "Kids Wilderness Survival" in case they get lost in the woods. Children may also borrow Junior Ranger Activity packets, which contain such necessities as magnifiers, collecting jars, a compass, and an activity book.

On the other hand, the Big Thicket Association also offers a variety of services on a continuous basis. Canoe trips with the association, for example, occur every week with nature studies and hikes into the Thicket not under the authority of the Preserve mandates. They also explore national forests to the north and west. The association's rustic museum in Saratoga displays insects, plants, and animals that are found in the Thicket, and you'll also learn about oil, lumber, rice, and beans, important sources of revenue in East Texas. There are walking trails and canoe trips, with qualified guides who live in the Big Thicket and know it thoroughly available for reasonable fees. Write for their newsletter that informs readers of Thicket folklore, history, and particulars about plant and animal life. If you go to Saratoga, be sure to stop and have a piece of homemade coconut pie at Poor Joe's Cafe across the street from the museum. You may even hear a few stories about the haunted "Saratoga lights" on the Old Ghost Road that cuts into the Thicket nearby.

A word of warning: Don't go into the Big Thicket until you have registered at the trailhead and, by all means, stay on the trail. Carry drinking water as creek water is not potable. And, if you want to be able to identify plants and animals, pick up a field guide and identification book at the museum or ask the park service to provide you with their brochures on the subjects that interest you.

Edison Plaza Museum

350 Pine Street
P.O. Box 3652
Beaumont 77704
409-839-2089
Hours: 8 a.m.–5 p.m., Mon.–Fri.
Admission free.
How to get there: Located in downtown Beaumont. Take Interstate 10
going east toward Lake Charles. Exit on Martin Luther King
Parkway and turn left on Caulder, which runs into Pine.

On the night of October 21, 1879, Thomas Edison had another of his endless brainstorms. He took a piece of cotton thread from his wife's sewing basket and soaked it in carbon. That piece of carbonized thread became the wondrous horseshoe-shaped filament in a clear glass bulb that lit the world. For Edison, this was just the beginning.

The Edison Plaza Museum is a hands-on experience designed to allow you to step into the mind of one of America's greatest inventors. Housed in Beaumont's old 1929 Gulf States Utilities Substation and governed by that company's board of directors, this is an exceptional electric industry museum, the only one of its kind in the South.

Museum curator Jill Street has traced inventions of the past, present, and future which led to Edison's own record 1,093 inventions. Under Ms. Street's direction, visitors can send messages to each other via telegraph keys, turn on a replica of Edison's first light, and exert enough energy to power two light bulbs, a small fan, and a small TV, by pedaling a bike.

Don't miss this museum. It's a fitting tribute to Thomas Edison and his remarkable talents.

Fire Museum of Texas

400 Walnut at Mulberry
Beaumont 77701
409-838-0619
Hours: 10 a.m.–4 p.m., Mon.–Fri.
Admission free.
How to get there: Located one block from the Edison Plaza Museum.

Here's your chance to slide down a fire pole and sit behind the wheel of a ladder truck. The firefighters here want you to experience their museum and hopefully grow to love their profession as much as they do. Located on the corner

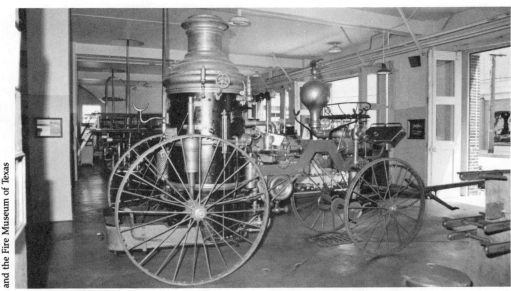

Photo courtesy of Fire Chief C. A. Shelton and the Fire Museum of Texas

This 1879 American Steamer is the focus of Beaumont's Fire Museum of Texas.

of Walnut and Mulberry, this great museum is quartered in the 1927 Beaumont Fire Department Headquarters Station, now a Texas Historical Landmark. Named "The Fire Museum of Texas" by the State Firemen's and Fire Marshals' Association, this is one museum you and your kids will remember.

Featured here is everything from an 1856 hand-drawn tub pumper to a 1909 American LaFrance Aerial ladder truck to the first search light truck built in 1931. Visitors are allowed to climb aboard the shiny, well-kept trucks, and there's even a special fire pole, actually used in the late forties, that pretend firefighters can slide down. You'll see a large collection of fire badges and helmets, and there's even a Japanese exhibit from Beppu City, Japan, Beaumont's sister city, where Japanese uniforms, badges, and helmets are in view. The children's favorites, though, are tombstones of dog heroes who gave their lives during the call of duty and of Major, a beloved firehorse.

The most creative display, though, is a working fire box, used in a time when phones were nonexistent and the accompanying Gamewell Fire Alarm System received the calls via a kind of Morse Code. When the curator pulls the lever, you'll actually see the message tapped out. Call ahead, however, for a scheduled tour. This way, you'll get a first hand explanation from a member of the Beaumont Fire Department.

Gladys City/Spindletop Museum

P.O. Box 10082
Beaumont 77710
409-880-8122
Hours: 1 p.m.–5 p.m., Sun.–Fri.; 9 a.m.–5 p.m. Sat.
Admission charged.

How to get there: Located at the intersection of University Drive and U.S. Highway 69-96-287

Beaumont has as its claim to fame Spindletop, the well that in 1901 signified the birth of big oil in Texas. The city payed tribute to this event by reconstructing Gladys City, Spindletop's boom town, as their Bicentennial project. Using the original "Gladys City" plans, builders reconstructed the old post office, saloon, broker's office, blacksmith shop, and a block of others to give visitors an idea of what life was like on the "Hill." Operated by Lamar University, Gladys City is filled with period antiques, and there are even oil derricks, similar to the ones used at the turn-of-the-century. Also here is the Lucas Gusher Monument, a 58-foot granite obelisk which is a National Historic Landmark commemorating the discovery of oil on Spindletop dome. You may also want to stop by the Spindletop Museum (955 East Florida on the Lamar University Campus, 409-838-9107. Admission is free.)

Brenham

The Blue Bell Creamery

FM 577
Brenham 77833
409-836-7977
Hours: 10 a.m. and then every 30 minutes from 1 p.m.–3 p.m., Mon.–Fri.; March–Oct.; 10 a.m. and 1:30 only, Mon.–Fri., Nov.–Feb.
Admission free.
How to get there: Located on FM 577, about two miles southeast of downtown Brenham. From US 290, turn north on FM 577 and go one mile.

Texans who have tasted Blue Bell Ice Cream think it's the best ice cream this side of paradise. Unfortunately, not all Texans can savor the taste of this scrumptious blend. Made

since 1911, "the little creamery at Brenham" distributes only in and around the areas of Beaumont, Houston, Austin, Dallas, San Antonio, and Brenham, of course. Supposedly, there's no secret to the recipe except that the creamery uses only good, fresh dairy products. But, no wonder it's good, as this "creme de la creme" delight is made up of 12 percent butterfat, which is 20 percent more than Blue Bell's competitors. Weight Watcher's Pat Walker would cringe at that fact, but the added calories will send you into pure ecstasy. With 40,000 cows supplying fresh milk to it daily, the creamery produces 22 flavors at a time, varying flavors like peach, blueberry, and strawberry when the fruit is in season.

Free tours, which end with a complimentary dip of Blue Bell, are conducted Mondays through Fridays and last about 45 minutes. This will be a treat for ice cream lovers everywhere and a special favorite for the kids.

Brookshire

Green Meadows Farm

Box 547
Brookshire 77423
713-391-7995
Hours: Tours are given Tuesday through Sunday, May through
October, at various times during the day according to the seasons.
Closed Nov.–April.
Admission charged.
How to get there: From Houston, travel I-10 west to Brookshire and
north on FM 359 to Green Meadows Farm.

Do you sometimes worry that the closest your children have ever been to a cow is the grocery dairy department, and you feel guilty because they've never had an opportunity to feed baby chicks or ride a horse?

Green Meadows Farms, forty miles west of downtown Houston, is in the business of parent redemption. A brainchild of Wisconsin farmers Cliff and Virginia Magness, the 50-acre spread addresses this problem by offering "hands-on" country experience. Though Green Meadows is an unlikely neighbor to one of the nation's largest cities, it's here that city children, particularly those of nursery and elementary school age, can touch and feed goats, sheep, turkeys, peacocks, pigs, and miniature horses. Visitors are given a two-hour tour in which everyone is actually allowed into the animal pens, which incidentally are kept meticulously clean. With supervision, kids actually hold hens, ducks, and baby pigs.

The stars of the show, however, seem to be the piglets who scamper from restricting arms every chance they get, only to cause giggles and screams as children scamper to catch the babies. Children are enthralled to learn that the tails of piglets are clipped off at an early age because they like to bite each other's off and male peacocks sprout a totally new set of colorful tail feathers every winter.

While the kids are milking "Miss Elsie," the dairy cow, or petting "Friday," the farm's 2,000 lb. Belgium horse, parents can relax under the trees. You'll need to wear your farm attire, though, because everyone goes on a hayride after all the children have a chance to ride ponies.

If you're a guest at the farm in October, your kids will be allowed to select their own Halloween pumpkin from hundreds hidden in the meadows. Reservations three weeks in advance are preferred. No food is served, but beverages are available via a soft drink machine. Bring your own lunch and sit under the farm's pavilion.

Galveston Island

Galveston Convention and Visitors Bureau

2106 Seawall Boulevard
Galveston 77550
TX Toll Free 1-800-351-4236
Nat'l Toll Free 1-800-351-4237
In Galveston, call 763-4311
How to get there: Located on Seawall Boulevard across from Hotel
Galvez.

Galveston Island, a Gulf of Mexico semi-tropical barrier island and one of Texas' most popular resort cities, is a lady with a past. Her beaches are not as white as those in Miami and her waters not as blue, but "the Island," as residents call her, has a charm that is irresistible, intertwined with legend, history, and colorful figures.

Though so many visitors leave Galveston without ever seeing much more than the oceanside and the island's formidable

17-foot, 10-mile long seawall, the "Oleander City" has a treasure chest full of attractions. Only 30 miles long and 1½ miles wide, this vacation spot could conceivably keep a vacationing family busy for an entire week without their ever setting foot on the beach. Museums, quaint shops, parks, and seafood restaurants abound, with Galveston's stormy history coming alive in every nook and cranny.

You'll hear about the Great Storm of 1900 that killed 6,000 people, prompted the building of the seawall, and resulted in the entire city having to be raised five feet. You'll marvel at the surviving 1,500 historic structures that tell of the city's gracious past and its people's indomitable will to survive. From your hotel, you're only a trolley ride away from the colorful Strand, a Historic Landmark District and Galveston's once bustling financial district known in the late 1800s as the "Wall Street of the Southwest."

You'll be entertained as well as educated and all along, you'll experience a calming serenity that comes only from being by the sea.

Be forewarned that although the island has a string of beachfront hotels and condominiums along Seawall Boulevard, make reservations well in advance. Beachhouses are also for rent on the west end of the Island in Pirate's Beach, Indian Beach, and Sea Isle. (For information on resort rentals, contact MRC Realty 409-737-2771.) Peak tourist times are the summer months, Mardi Gras, the historic homes tour in May, and the first weekend in December when the annual event, "Dickens-on-the-Strand" occurs. Keep in mind also that the luxurious Tremont Hotel is located on the Strand and provides guests with the best accommodations money can buy. In addition, many "bed-and-breakfast" accommodations in turn-of-the-century homes in the "Silk Stocking" district and along Broadway, are also available; but not all accept children.

Galveston Beaches

Minimal parking fees charged

The island has 32 miles of beautiful public beaches, billed as "the cleanest on the Texas Gulf Coast." These municipally maintained shorelines are also the safest as the Galveston County Sheriff's Department Beach Patrol posts lifeguards in designated areas and provides safety and rescue services. However, the sea commands respect with its currents and uneven bottom that can take even an experienced swimmer out to sea. Teach your kids the rules, follow the posted signs, stay close to shore, and swim safe distances from piers and pilings. This way, you'll have a great time in Galveston waters.

Though all of the Galveston beaches are for public use, every area, of course, has something different to offer. The closer you get to the east end of the island, the more populated the beaches become. The more family-oriented beach park seems to be Stewart Beach Park, located at the junc-

ture of Broadway (Interstate 45) and Seawall Boulevards. Operated by the City of Galveston Park Board of Trustees, the park features a new pavilion with gift shops, concessions, restaurants, and a large bath house. Adjacent to the park are a carnival and water slide, bumper boats and cars, go carts, miniature golf and amusement rides. Although this beach is always crowded, it is by far the kids' favorite. Chair, float, and umbrella rentals are also available (for more information on Stewart Beach, call 409-765-5023). Along the boulevard tourists can rent bicycles, roller skates, surreys as well as rafts and surfboards. (Be sure to take the kids to Kites, Etc., a unique little shop that carries both stunt and single-line kites of all colors and sizes. It's located at 57th and Seawall Boulevard.) Since there is no railing on the seawall, you may want to ride or skate nearest the edge so you can give your life for your child if the need arises!

If you still want to be close to the east side of Galveston but don't need all the added attractions, try Apffel Park, another city recreation spot, just east of Stewart Beach. This one is popular with fishermen and teenagers. The facility offers a bath house, public restrooms, concessions, and a gift shop as well as a boat launch, jetty, and surf fishing facilities (call 409-763-0166). There are no RV hookups here, but if you brought your camper try Dellanera RV Park, also under the jurisdiction of the city park division, which is equipped with 50 full hookups, bathroom facilities, laundry, grocery store and pavilion. Located on the west end at 7 Mile Road and FM 3005, Dellanera Park offers a long, quiet stretch of shoreline with camping fees averaging $12 per night and $3 per day per car (409-740-0390).

On the west side of the island is Galveston Island State Park, a 2,000-acre park with 1.6 miles of beach with 170 campsites and 10 screened shelters. Located about 9 miles west of 61st Street or 1 mile west of 13-Mile Road, this park has a 4-mile nature trail with observation platforms, bird viewing blinds, and boardwalks over existing bayous. For information, write Galveston Island State Park, Route 1, Box 156-A, Galveston, Texas 77551 or phone 409-737-1222.

Whatever you do, stay out of the sun during the peak hours because mid-day rays can wreak havoc by causing heat stroke and sunburn for fair-skinned beach lovers. Even on cloudy days, sunburn can occur, so use caution. Caution your kids not to touch the jelly fish. Even dead ones on the beach can sting.

The Bolivar Ferry

Ferry Road (State Highway 87)
Galveston Ferry Operations Department of Highways and Public
  Transportation
P.O. Box 381
Galveston 77553-0381
409-763-2386
Admission free.
How to get there: Head east on Seawall Boulevard; turn left on 2nd
  Street (Ferry Road), which deadends at the ferry landing.

The Bolivar Ferry is the best free ride in Galveston and offers a great view of the harbor traffic.

A good way to spend the morning or afternoon is to be the guest of the Texas Department of Highways and Public Transportation by taking the twenty-minute ferry ride across Galveston's harbor over to Port Bolivar, the mainland's long peninsula. The ride gives you a great view of the harbor, passing ships and leisure craft, Seawolf Park, and local wildlife.

If you have any stale bread, bring it along to feed the seagulls that flock around the ferry. Unless you want to have your summer whites soiled, however, I suggest you feed them at the back of the boat with the wind at your back.

The observation deck is my favorite spot because it makes me feel like Barbra Streisand rushing through New York harbor in hot pursuit of Nicky Armstein. Aside from a "conquer-the-world" feeling, though, it will give you a better chance at spotting an occasional dolphin as it races with the ferry.

There are four ferries that run every twenty minutes during the day, and at night at specific hours only. Summer weekends, particularly holiday ones, make for a *long* wait. However, you can park your car and board the ferry on foot if you wish.

If you have your car when you get to Bolivar, drive one mile down Hwy 87 and see the Port Bolivar Lighthouse on the left, built in 1872. Now privately owned and not open to the public, the Bolivar Lighthouse was one of the first two erected in Texas. Seven feet tall and four feet wide, the lens that was housed here is now on display at the Smithsonian Institute. You can see its twin taken from the South Jetty Lighthouse in the Galveston County Historical Museum.

The Strand

How to get there: Located on the north side of the Island, a block off the port. The restored district can be found primarily between 20th and 25th (Rosenberg) streets.

The Strand, formerly the wealthiest commercial center west of the Mississippi, was dubbed the "Wall Street of the Southwest" in its late 19th-century heyday. Situated in the heart of one of Texas' busiest seaports, this once-sophisticated banking and investment center became the birthplace for many fortunes, rooted in cotton, finance, and shipping.

The 1900 storm and the subsequent rebuilding of the entire city put Galveston behind her peers. Coupled with the Depression, the Strand began to feel the effects of financial decline and after a time, became nothing other than a string of deserted streets full of memories.

With the help of the Galveston Historical Foundation and diehard supporters of the city, the Strand is now experiencing a renaissance, alive again with quaint shops, galleries, museums and the fabulous 1894 Grand Opera House. This is also the site of the city's Christmas celebration "Dickens-on-the-Strand," a lavish event which occurs the first weekend in December (see *The Best of Texas Festivals*, Lone Star Books, 1986).

If you don't want to drive, catch a trolley and get off at Strand and 21st streets. This will put you only a few steps from The Strand Visitors Center, 2016 Strand (409-765-7834 or 713-488-5942). Manned by the historical foundation in the old 1859 Hendley Building, the people there can help you find your way about, and you can also buy tickets here for many of the visitor attractions. Don't miss **Col. Bubbies Strand Surplus Senter** (2202 Strand). A gigantic warehouse filled with every kind of military memoribilia imaginable, it's the place to go to see a real ejection seat close up and to buy those Spanish saddle bags you've always wanted.

The *Elissa*

Pier 21, one block off The Strand
Galveston 77551
Hours: 10 a.m.–5 p.m. weekdays (extended hours Sat. and Sun.)
409-763-0027, Galveston; 713-488-5942, Houston.
Admission charged.
How to get there: Located at the end of 23rd Street at Pier 21.

The *Elissa*, Texas' "tall ship," was resurrected in 1974 from a Greek scrapyard by the Galveston Historical Foundation, who renewed portions of her hull, towed her to America, and then completely restored her. Thanks to the Foundation, she is now open seven days a week to the public for self-guided tours.

The *Elissa*, 200-feet-long and boasting a main mast that towers more than 100 feet above the deck, has a vivid history that began with her launch from a Scottish builder's yard in 1877. Among her many voyages, the square-rigger visited such ports-of-call as Calcutta, Tampico, and twice to Galveston. She eventually wound up in the hands of Greek smugglers.

For many years, the *Elissa*, minus her sailing rig, remained in disrepair in a Pireaus, Greece, shipyard until she was purchased by the Foundation for $40,000. In 1986, she represented Galveston and Texas at the Statue of Liberty Centennial Celebration by sailing at the end of the Class A Tall Ships. The iron barque *Elissa* was the oldest of her class and the only restored 19th-century square-rigger in the parade of sails.

Photo courtesy of the Galveston Historical Foundation

The Elissa, *Galveston's historical 1877 square-rigger and Texas' "tall ship," is open to the public seven days a week.*

The Galveston County Historical Museum

2219 Market Street
Galveston 77550
409-766-2340
Hours: 9 a.m.–4 p.m., Mon.–Sat., 1 p.m.–5 p.m., Sun., summers, 9
a.m.–4 p.m., Mon.–Fri., 11 a.m.–4 p.m., Sat.; closed Sun; winters.
Admission free.
How to get there: From the beach, turn north on 23rd Street. Cross
Broadway to Market Street. Turn right on Market and stop. The
museum's raised entrance sits back from the building facade.

The Galveston County Historical Museum, a project of the Galveston Historical Foundation and the Galveston Commissioners Court, depicts life as it existed on the Island, its surrounding mainland, and the Bolivar Pennisula from prehistoric times to the present. Visitors can marvel at the priceless beauty of the crystal lens taken from the old South Jetty Lighthouse and kids can climb on an 1836 cannon from the Navy ship *Brutus*. A. L. Bogotto's General Store brought in tact from Dickinson, Texas, occupies the first floor, and the changing exhibits such as on works of the famous 19th-century architect, Nicholas Clayton, on the construction of the Galveston Seawall, and the glittering gowns from Mardi Gras celebrations.

The Railroad Museum

Center for Transportation and Commerce
25th & Strand Street
Galveston 77550
409-765-5700
Hours: 10 a.m.–5 p.m., daily.
Admission charged.
How to get there: Located in the Strand at the west end of Strand
Street.

If the lonesome whistle of a distant locomotive reminds you of nostalgic times, then chug along to the Railroad Museum (formerly called Center for Transportation and Commerce), home of the largest collection of restored rail cars and locomotives in the Southwest United States. You won't have to reminisce from a distance as visitors are actually allowed to board Pullman cars, steam locomotives, mail cars, coaches and diners.

Don't miss the working model of the Port of Galveston featuring HO-gauge model trains, pulling cargo from the world to Galveston rail terminals. Small children can actually crawl under the scale model and poke their heads up into plastic viewing circles that give them a giant's-eye view of all the action. There's also a small carpeted arena where you can sit and rest while the kids have fun.

The best is yet to come, however, when visitors step back in time by entering The People's Gallery, the authentic Santa Fe Depot Waiting Room. There you'll find 32 stark white plastered "apparitions" who have somehow been caught in a kind of time warp. Frozen sculptures in authentic 1932 clothing, these works of art were created by Ivan and Elliott Schwartz. By picking up "hearphones" adjacent to the sculptures, you can even eavesdrop on the conversations and thoughts of these ghostly travelers.

If you have older kids with you, plan to have "Dinner (or lunch) . . . On the Diner," which is an actual 1930s' dining car where cuisine is served in the true train travel tradition. And if you're planning to be in Galveston on holiday weekends, call about the short steam excursions offered for $1. You might also call to see if any events are planned for kids. On occasion, the museum sponsors Hobo parties where kids spend the night and cook Mulligan stew.

The Colonel Paddlewheeler

2209 Strand
Galveston 77550
409-763-4666 (Houston: 713-280-3980)
Admission charged. (Prices run about $8 for adults, $4 for kids 4–12,
and kids under 4 free.)
How to get there: Take 25th (Rosenberg) to the docks. The Colonel is
docked off 22nd Street at Pier 22 next to the Elissa.

If you've always wanted to ride a riverboat down the Mississippi in the true Mark Twain tradition, but you're not going to New Orleans any time soon, you're in luck. Galveston has its own rendition of the classic vessel—*The Colonel*, the Moody Foundation's 325-ton diesel-powered paddlewheeler, which takes tourists for day and nighttime cruises.

Actually, paddlewheelers are no stranger to the Island. In the glory days before the Great Storm of 1900 when seaport tonnage was at its height, these romantic sternwheelers, with their triple decks and Victorian finery were a common sight along Galveston shores. So, to accommodate the increasing numbers to one of Texas' most historic and oldest cities, *The Colonel*, 150 feet long and 40 feet wide, was specially ordered from a New Orleans paddlewheeler builder. Now, visitors to the Island can ride the 19th-century-styled riverboat even in the off-season months.

There are two daily bay cruises, narrated by the captain. Hot dogs and drinks, including alcoholic beverages, are served on board. Arrive 30 minutes early to ensure that you'll get a good seat on the open-air promenade deck upstairs. Otherwise, you'll have to sit inside—air-conditioned and very comfortable—but not the kids' favorite.

If you decide to stay at the beach all day, a perfect way to end the evening is to take the dinner/jazz cruise complete with Dixieland band. This excursion leaves at 7 p.m. and returns to dock at 9 p.m.

Sea-Arama/Marineworld

Seawall Blvd. & 91st
P.O. Box 3068
Galveston 77552
409-744-4501 (Houston: 713-488-4441).
Hours: 10 a.m.–7 p.m., daily, year round.
Admission charged. (Children under 4 admitted free. Senior citizens
*   and children 4–12 eligible for reduced rates.)*
How to get there: Go west on Seawall Boulevard and take a right on
*   91st Street.*

Sea-Arama, the home of some very talented animals, will probably be what the kids remember about their trip to Galveston. Located on the west end of Seawall Boulevard, this 38-acre complex full of tropical landscaping provides a natural setting for everything from parrots to piranhas. Dolphin, bird, sea lion, shark, and ski shows take place all through the day though it's a good idea to call about the times first if you want to see a specific one.

The heart of Sea-Arama is a fascinating 200,000 gallon oceanarium where a fearless scuba diver hand-feeds man-eating sharks once in the morning and once in the late afternoon. This is always a favorite among the little children. Another favorite is the humorous bird show, which occurs at 1:30 p.m. and 4:45 p.m. only. You'll meet such characters as Captain Harvey, a white cockatoo who salutes every time he's introduced, Dottie, a blue and yellow macaw who cries for help in a Southern accent, and 76-year-old Barnacle Butch, a red macaw hatched in 1911.

Seawolf Park

Pelican Island
City of Galveston Park Board of Trustees
2106 Seawall Boulevard
Galveston 77550
409-744-5738
Admission charged.
How to get there: Go north on 51st Street (Seawolf Parkway) from
*   Broadway, which will take you over the bridge that connects Pelican*
*   Island to Galveston.*

Named after the *USS Seawolf*, a Naval sub that sank 27 enemy ships and damaged 13, Seawolf Park was proposed by the U.S. Submarine Veterans of World War II to honor the 3,505 submariners lost during the war.

You'll be able to explore the *USS Cavalla* and the *USS Stewart* as well as an M23 Tank and QF-86H fighter bomber. Called "The Luckiest Ship in the Submarine Service" during World War II, the *Cavalla* sank 34,180 tons of Japanese ships, including a loaded aircraft carrier that participated in the attack on Pearl Harbor.

The *Stewart*, a destroyer-escort, was scuttled and captured by the Japanese who refloated it and re-outfitted it for active duty. By the end of World War II the persistent rumor of an enemy ship "that looks like one of ours" was proven to be true when the U.S. Navy discovered the *USS Stewart* in Japan after the war.

You can board the vessels which means climbing up ladders, elbowing through hatches and making your way

Dolphins delight old and young as they leap and dive in a game of waterball at SeaArama.

The USS Stewart, a World War II destroyer escort captured by the Japanese and then reclaimed by the Navy at the war's end, sits on display at Seawolf Park.

through tight quarters. That means you'll be better off wearing tennis shoes and lightweight clothing in the summer.

You may want to consider picnicking on Pelican Island. The view is out to open sea and there are tables and benches for that purpose as well as playground equipment for the kids. If you want to fish or crab, you can use the public pier that takes you out into deeper water. Regulars here tell of speckled trout, flounder, and sometimes red fish being caught from it. If fishing sounds like fun, but you don't have your gear, don't despair. The little bait camp at the beginning of the pier rents rods and reels and sells bait and ice.

Whatever you do, though, bring mosquito repellent in case the wind is blowing the wrong way.

Train and Trolley Tours

Treasure Island Tour Train
21st and Seawall
Galveston 77550
409-765-9564
Hours: 9 a.m., 11 a.m., 1:30 p.m., 3:30 p.m. in May with an additional 5:30 tour scheduled from June–August. Fall, winter and spring tours are 11 a.m. and 1:30 p.m. Closed Mondays. Closed Jan.–Feb.
Admission charged.
How to get there: Located on the corner of 21st and Seawall Boulevard at the Convention and Visitors Bureau in the Moody Center across from Hotel Galvez.

After you've had a chance to spend some time at the beach, take the opportunity to see Galveston on an orga-

nized tour. You have two choices. The first, more extensive one, which lasts about 1½ hours, covers 17 miles around Galveston Island via a 64-passenger open-air tour train. This fun ride takes you to both old and new Galveston, including Seawall Boulevard, the business district, historic homes, the Yacht Basin, the University of Texas Medical Branch, and places of interest in between. Passengers hear about the early days of Galveston, the 1900 Storm, and the city's gambling days before the grand entrance of the Texas Rangers in the late fifties. The extensive commentary tells you just about everything. If you have older kids, take this one. If you have pre-schoolers, consider the trolley tour instead. It's shorter and faster and has something all little ones like—a real trolley bell.

The Galveston Flyer
The Strand Visitors Center
2016 Strand
Galveston 77550
409-763-0884
Hours: Departures hourly from 21st Street and Seawall Blvd. and on the half-hour from 21st and Strand.
Admission charged.

The *Galveston Flyer*, a unique, hand-built replica of a c. 1900 American trolley, runs a continuous circuit between 21st and Seawall Boulevard to the Railroad Museum along the Strand and to the east beach area. It, too, gives a historic commentary but with less detail. The children have great fun on the trolley, because they are allowed to stand at the back of the trolley outside the cab.

Houston and Vicinity

Greater Houston Convention and Visitors Council
3300 Main St.
Houston

Houston, Texas' most colossal city, pulsates with the sounds of people on the move. For the tourist not afraid to conquer the tangle of freeways, it will provide you and your family with an endless number of exciting attractions.

One of the main things to note about the city is that Loop 610 will get you to any major freeway. So, plan your route before you leave for the day and allow yourself plenty of travel time. Remember also that in Houston, as is in any major city, you'll have a better time if you stay off the freeways between the peak traffic hours of 6 a.m. to 9 a.m. and 4 p.m. to 6:30 p.m. Also keep in mind that you'll find major tourist favorites like Astroworld and Hermann Park won't be as crowded during the week.

The first thing you need to do, particularly if you plan to drive on the 300 miles of freeway system, is call or write the Greater Houston Convention and Visitors Council. They'll be happy to send you their comprehensive tourist guide that includes maps of Houston, its environs and whatever brochures (there are 300 in all) you request.

Downtown Houston

Don't let downtown Houston overwhelm you. It's an exciting city with such a distinctive skyline it provides architectural students with a complete showcase of form and design. Time, talent and the open mind have flourished with historic buildings of Old Market Square and Sam Houston Park co-existing within the shadows of dramatic contemporary highrises. The result has been the eclectic "Space City," a perfect blend of the past, present and future.

In order to explore its many faces, however, you really need to brave the freeways, head downtown, park and walk. This way you're sure to see the many waterfalls, complementing building designs, the flowering corporate plazas and the contemporary art sculptures that will spur lively, and sometimes heated, conversation. If you don't want to drive, the Metro buses run throughout the day from downtown to outer urban areas. For information call 713-635-4000.

The American Institute of Architects Tour of Downtown Buildings

Meet in the lobby of the downtown Hyatt Regency
713-622-2081
Hours: 2 p.m., the third Sunday of each month.
Admission charged (reservations required).

Conducted by a local architect, this is an hour-and-45-minute narrated stroll with no refreshment or bathroom stops. The tour is very informative, particularly if you have an aspiring architect in your midst. You'll not only hear stories about these fantastic skyscrapers but also learn a little about the people who built them. Unless your child is intrigued with projecting entranceways, balustrades, and rolled parapets, I would spare them.

Greater Houston Preservation Alliance Downtown Walking Tour

Meet at the corner of Milam and Preston
Hours: Noon, the third Wednesday of every month.
Donation requested.

This is a guided 45-minute walking tour of buildings dating from 1847–1915 in the Market Square.

Self-Guided Walking Tours

Because neither guided tour takes you inside any structure, plan your own excursion on a weekday when all the buildings are open. Tourists are allowed on the sky lobby levels of the Allied Bank Plaza and the Texas Commerce Tower (600 Travis; Monday through Friday 7 a.m.–7 p.m.; wheelchair access), the tallest building in the state at 75 stories and 1,002 feet. From the sixtieth-floor of the Texas Commerce Tower, you'll see the Gothic-spired Republic Bank building to the northwest as well as the two black Pennzoil Place trapezoids that cut into the skyline. To the west is Heritage Plaza, a reflective glass structure which has been described as a building whose "surface strips away like a banana peel near the top to reveal an ornamental topping reminiscent of a Mayan ceremonial temple."

For another view of Houston's skyline, and in my opinion the most spectacular, take the Allied Bank Plaza elevator and fly skyward up to the fifty-ninth floor where the two-level observatory faces east and south. This one is absolutely breath-taking. (1000 Louisiana, enter on Louisiana between McKinney and Lamar; Monday through Friday, 7 a.m.–7 p.m., Saturday and Sunday, 8 a.m.–1 p.m.)

Downtown Tunnel System

If it's raining or nippy, and you don't want to walk outside, you can take the downtown tunnel system, a very clean and well-lit subterranean walkway that connects to all the major buildings in a nine-block square. Called the largest tunnel system of its kind in the world, this five-mile labyrinth began to grow 35 years ago bit by bit until today it meanders under more than 70 percent of all downtown office space. All the buildings involved have their own escalator or elevator entrances, though the one at the Hyatt Regency will take you near the underground Park Lane Cafeteria. The tunnel is full of eating places and cheerful little shops.

Downtown Parks

Besides Hermann Park, Houston has a surprising number of parks located in close vicinity to the downtown area. The first, Sam Houston Historical Park at Bagby and McKinney Streets across from City Hall, is the oldest in Houston. After you finish your lunch, walk over to the park's historic homes and a replica of Houston when it was just a village. This is a great place to rest your weary feet because it's shady in spots, and the steep slope of the land delights and challenges the more energetic and daring little people with you.

Within ten minutes from downtown by car, you can reach Memorial Park, the joggers' jungle. Go west on Memorial Drive and you're there (if you hit Loop 610, you've gone too far). You'll find yourself in a wooded setting with picnic tables, playground equipment and, most important, bathrooms, totally in conflict with the space age steel skyscrapers only a short distance away. Further down, closer to the Loop, is Aline McAshan Botanical Gardens and Arboretum at 4500 Woodway. A natural habitat, the arboretum is filled with many varieties of wildflowers, shrubs and trees. A boardwalk runs through the habitats of bullfrogs, crickets, water snakes, and the giant red-headed woodpecker. If you

go here, spend a little time with the kids in the Discovery Room, where microscopes are set up to examine snake skins and spider eggs. The children will also see fresh water catfish in a huge aquarium, learn about the different kinds of pine cones and pick up and feel real turtle shells.

The Houston Fire Museum

2403 Milam
Houston 77006
409-524-2526
Hours: 10 a.m.–4 p.m., Tues.–Sat.
Admission free.
How to get there: Exit at McKinney Street from I-45 and then turn right on Milam, a one-way street going south.

At The Houston Fire Museum, volunteer firemen demonstrate how the vanishing street corner fire alarm boxes work. In addition, they explain the particulars about 1893 Water Tower No. 1, the oldest truck in the museum and the LaFrance 1923 Pumper with the steering wheel on the right hand side, giving the driver easy access to other controls. You'll learn a bit of trivia, too, such as the fact that truck ladders are still wooden to protect against electrical shock.

Upstairs, the kids will see the actual locker room used for years by firemen stationed at No. 7, a badge display, memorabilia from the famous Texas City fire, a collection of brass hoses and fire helmets, and a set of antique fire grenades. Upon request, visitors may also see a video of some of the major Houston fires as well as a cartoon on fire prevention. The video works wonders to discourage children who are fascinated with matches.

The Houston Zoo

1513 Outer Belt Drive
Houston 77030
713-523-5888
Hours: 10 a.m.–6 p.m. Closed Mondays.
Admission free.
How to get there: Located in Hermann Park off the 6300 block of Fannin.

Pick up a map at the Houston Zoo's entrance and chart your course before you begin sightseeing. Take it from someone who's been lost in the zoo with a tearful, tired child, it's easy to get turned around once you enter the gates. The zoo also rents the big kind of strollers that will accommodate those children too big for baby strollers but easily tired when having to walk long distances.

I suggest that if you have small children, head first toward the children's petting zoo (which closes at 4 p.m.), located at the very back of the park and work your way back.

On your way back from the children's zoo, stop by and stare at the African gorillas, who'll be gawking back at you, in a steaming jungle habitat. And don't miss the hippos, alligators, and the elephants who live near each other on the west side of the complex. If the kids are hot and sweaty by this time, go into any one of the air-conditioned buildings, such as the small mammal house where you can examine vampire bats or the wonderful Kipp Aquarium full of fresh and saltwater inhabitants. Also a must is the jungle bird house patterned after the ruins of a Mayan Temple.

A great way to end your zoo excursion is to ride the miniature train that takes you for a pleasant ride through the park. For a small fee, you not only can get a good idea of where you might want to picnic, but the kids will love it. I'll bet you a train ticket they'll ask you if they can ride a second time.

I strongly suggest you bring your own lunch. There are picnic tables set up all around the park and there's an abundance of shade. The park also has some popular playground equipment located near the pavilion, close to Fannin Boulevard. Save the crust of your sandwiches so the kids can feed the ducks, who live around the lake. (By the way, children can fish here, so bring a pole.)

The Houston Museum of Natural Science/Burke Baker Planetarium

1 Hermann Circle Drive
Hermann Park
Houston 77030
713-526-4273
Hours: 9 a.m.–5 p.m., Tues.–Sat.; 12 p.m.–5 p.m., Sun.–Mon.
Admission charged.
How to get there: Located in Hermann Park off Fannin. Take a right on Hermann Circle Drive. The statue of Sam Houston will be your landmark.

The first question my son always asks when he hears we're going to a museum is "Do they have any dinosaur bones?" In our family, the number of dinosaur bones displayed in any given museum is the measuring stick of quality.

The Houston Museum of Natural Science not only has dinosaur bones, but it has a 70-foot-long genuine honest-to-goodness diplodocus skeleton, two stories tall, that greets wide-eyed visitors as soon as they enter the door.

Photo courtesy of the Museum of Natural Science

This 70-foot-long diplodocus skeleton greets every visitor to Houston's Museum of Natural Science.

Next to the diplodocus, you'll also see the head of a tyrannosaurus rex and a replica of an ankylosaurus.

Other attractions include a petroleum science and technology wing, an Indian exhibit containing Geronimo's war club, a space center, the incredible gem and mineral exhibit, and the Hall of Medical Science in which children can play computer games all relating to health.

Suggest to your kids that they save their vacation money so they can spend it here where there's a great gift shop full of educational games, models, and books.

The 232-seat Burke Baker Planetarium, housed within the same building, provides programing throughout the year for child and adult star-gazers alike. Call for times and scheduled events.

The Children's Museum of Houston

3201 Allen Parkway
Houston 77019
713-52-AMUSE
Hours: 10 a.m.–5 p.m., Tues., Wed., and Sat.; 1 p.m.–5 p.m., Thurs. and Sun. Closed Mon. and Fri.
Admission charged.
How to get there: Take Allen Parkway toward town. Turn right on Waugh Drive.

Down one wall, refrigerator doors stand proudly displaying the creations of some of Houston's best child artists. Give the little people in your family a chance to create, explore, experience—at the Children's Museum. This unique "hands-on" museum, geared for ages 3–12, is based on the participatory concept whereby children learn by doing. As a result, kids play hard here, learning something in the process.

At the entrance, colorful hats on figures signifying different occupations from a fireman to a Houston Astro draw kids inside. The faces are eye-level mirrors which enable children to see themselves wearing the hats. Pretty creative stuff, you say?

This is only the beginning. The staff also wants to promote a better understanding among peoples. The museum's "Oaxaca Village" is the facility's answer to Old Mexico, where kids dress in Mexican sombreros while they grind corn, bargain in the marketplace, and weave a basket. And your whiz kids will love the computer center where they can participate in "me-you" computer communication exchange and draw on computer screens with light pens. In the Recycle Center, underwritten by Coca-Cola Foods, children create masterpieces which they can take home from styrofoam, milk cartons, and scrap yarn.

The best part of the museum, however, is the miniature Safeway store where children push kid-size baskets down aisles of pretend produce, can goods and dairy products. Each person, given a grocery list (with pictures and words), is encouraged to shop for those items. Once they've checked out, each has an opportunity to play the part of the

checker and the sacker. This exhibit seems to be the favorite of pre-schoolers and those of elementary age.

Though most of the exhibits are permanent, some travel from museum to museum, so you'll always find something new. So plan to spend an afternoon here where kids can have a ball and learn at the same time.

The Astrodome

Loop 610 and Kirby Drive
P.O. Box 288
Houston 77001
713-799-9544
Hours: 11 a.m., 1 p.m., 3 p.m. daily except on event days.
Admission charged. (Parking is about $3 and tour fees average $3 per person. Children under 6 get in free.)
How to get there: Take Loop 610 South. Exit Kirby Drive and go north. Enter at Gate 2.

The Houston Astrodome, home of the Astros and the Houston Oilers and still billed as the eighth wonder of the world, fits "Space City." It resembles a gigantic flying saucer that looks like it could swallow a small town in one gulp. Completed at the cost of $31.6 million in 1965, it was unveiled as the world's first all-weather, multipurpose stadium, and has acted as a role model for every other sports arena since. If you've never been to the Astrodome, try to make it for a game when the arena comes alive with excitement. The 52,000 seat stadium is under the jurisdiction of the Houston Sports Association, which offers one-hour tours on days no events are scheduled.

You'll see the elegant club rooms, the press box, and the super boxes, reserved for high-rollers. The added attraction is that the kids will get a chance to go down on the astro turf if the team is not practicing as well as see the animated scoreboard lit, complete with fireworks and raging bull. A ten-minute video is also shown about the stadium's past.

AstroWorld

9001 Kirby
Houston 77054
713-799-8404
Hours: Opens 10 a.m. Closing times vary. Closed Mondays. Open summer and some weekends during fall and spring.
Admission charged. (Parking is about $3.)
How to get there: Take Loop 610 South and exit at Kirby. The park is to the south of 610.

AstroWorld, the home of the Texas Cyclone, the world's number one roller coaster, is a theme park well worth a day's vacation. This Houston-based Six Flags facility covers 75 acres, and thematically represents 12 different countries.

Photo courtesy of AstroWorld/WaterWorld

AstroWorld's Texas Cyclone is heralded as the world's number one roller coaster.

Whatever you do, be sure to time your trip to catch the flag-waving, pride-bursting Great American Fireworks and Laser Spectacular show that occurs around 9:30 p.m. on summer nights. The night sky literally explodes with the full array of color to the sound of patriotic music.

If you're staying at a nearby hotel and have a few days to devote to AstroWorld, however, plan to go to the park after 4 p.m. and stay until closing. AstroWorld gives a free pass to anybody who buys a ticket after 4 p.m. on certain week days. Call or write, though, to make sure the policy is still in effect. In this way, you can return the next day at no additional charge.

AstroWorld has more than its share of thrills, including the Looping Star Ship, a mechanical wonder that suspends its passengers upside down and Thunder River, a man-made river ride with a raft that propels you and your group through whirlpools, waterfalls, canyons, lakes, and stair-step rapids.

Small children will love Enchanted Kingdom, billed as a "little people's paradise." There are slides, trampolines, and mazes plus the traditional kiddie rides. Enchanted Kingdom is also a frequent hang-out of such celebrities as Daffy Duck, Yosemite Sam, and Bugs Bunny. Check Houston papers for the special events frequently planned in this area. Also a very nice nursery is available to guests who need to change baby's diaper in peace. It also has a rocker and individualized rooms where you can quiet a fretful infant.

No coolers are allowed in the gate, but the park has fast food restaurants around every corner. If you plan to visit AstroWorld in the hot summer, the best time to go is late afternoon. Be sure to find out in advance when the U.S. High Diving Team Show, and shows at Enchanted Kingdom, the Texas Cow Palace, and Showcase Theatre are scheduled. Purchase a park map to help you plan your route and schedule.

WaterWorld

9001 Kirby
Houston 77054
713-799-1234
Hours: Opens 10 a.m. Closing times vary. Open every day in the
summer, weekends in May, and Labor Day weekend.
Admission charged.
How to get there: Located next to AstroWorld.

A day at WaterWorld is a day at the beach, only without the salt and the sand. Slide down "The Edge," an 80-foot free fall slide and see how it feels to be a bird swooping down only to skim the water's surface. You can bet your teenagers will try it. Once they've gone over "The Edge," it'll be a cinch for them to conquer "Wipe-out," the 300-foot speed slide that sends riders down a slide and zips them across a glistening pool of water at speeds of up to forty miles per hour.

That's not all! Kids will stand in line to master the "Hurricane," the "Typhoon," the "Tidal Wave" and the "Pipeline," four body slides that spiral and twist into corkscrew configurations that will send young hearts up into their throats.

If all this is not exactly your speed, try relaxing on an inner tube in the "Main Stream," a 900-foot-long river that lulls you with its soothing current. Or, if you wish, watch your "little squirts" have a ball in "Squirt's Splash," a fantasy water playground designed exclusively for children. Activities include a giant water maze, a hand-over-water course, two water slides, water cannons, swings, and the over-the-water rope bridge.

Life jackets are provided free of charge. Park officials strongly recommend that children and weak swimmers wear them. I highly recommend this also, particularly if you swim in the "Breaker Beach," a 30,000 square foot wave pool that produces a steady surge of four-foot waves. Though there are sufficient life guards, they can't possibly watch every child every second.

The food served here is a step above the usual amusement park cuisine. WaterWorld serves the most wonderful giant-sized ice creams in homemade waffle cones that are enough to feed two preschoolers or fill up one teenager. One other hint—bring some adhesive bandages for stumped toes and skinned knees, just in case. The park provides lockers for a small fee so lock up your valuables and go have a "waterworld" of fun.

Fame City

13700 Beechnut
Houston 77083
713-530-FAME
Hours: Opens at 10 a.m., daily in the summer; Open Fri., Sat. and
Sun. the rest of the year. Hours vary. Call for updated information.
Admission into individual attractions charged.
How to get there: Located one mile south of State Highway 6 at the
Beechnut crossing. Take Interstate 10 west. Turn left at Highway 6
(Addicks exit) and go left, then left at Beechnut.

Photo courtesy of Fame City

Families can do everything from bowl to ride the bumper cars at Fame City, Houston's indoor amusement park.

Fame City, a $40 million new amusement park concept is the answer for a family who wants to do it all. Enclosed in air-conditioned comfort, the sprawling facility has everything from a 40-lane bowling alley to a skating rink to every video game known to kids. While your older children go off to play "Wizard's Challenge" with its two 18-hole miniature golf courses or ride the fast-moving, strobe-lite Flash Flight Laser Ride, you can watch the smaller kids play in the slide-and-climb 10,000 square foot complex called Treasure Island. If you don't have little ones, you can take in one of the three Fame City cinemas or play Whirlyball, a ball game played in "Whirlybug" bumper cars.

There's free parking and admission into the park itself. However, nothing in life is really free, right? Once you enter, I suggest that you and your family walk around first and discover what each price package has to offer before you purchase one. The decision is going to be a tough one particularly if you have more than one child to please, so be prepared.

You'll need two things when you visit Fame City—socks and a pocketful of quarters. You'll need the socks if you plan to bowl or roller skate. The quarters . . . well . . . this place is the ultimate in videomania. Actually, there are so many other attractions, you could spend the entire day without having to feed a single machine, but the temptation here is great, particularly if these flashing monsters have a hypnotic effect on your offspring.

If you're claustraphobic, don't ride SR2, an airtight space-like capsule that simulates such thrilling scenes as driving a race car or riding a roller coaster. It's great fun and lasts only a few minutes, but once you're in, that's the point of no return! Also, if you're tired of eating hot dogs, try the bowling alley restaurant. Besides kid favorites, they also serve salads.

Fame City Waterworks

13700 Beechnut
Houston 77083
713-530-FAME
Hours: Opens at 10 a.m., daily in the summer.
Admission charged.
How to get there: Located adjacent to Fame City.

If it's a summer day and you just don't want to be inside, consider Waterworks, Fame City's answer to today's waterpark. The complex has a wave pool, complete with simulated oceanic waves, a slide that drops you 300 feet into the water at speeds of up to 40 miles per hour, and body slides that make complex twisting configurations 50 feet high.

The shallow area, designed for small children and fearful adults, contains water cannons, slides, a swing, a water maze, and a kiddie car wash. Parents can enjoy the 2,300-square-foot shaded area nearby. For a truly relaxing time, drift along in the Lazy River that circles the park. Waterworks furnishes life jackets free of charge and rents rafts and inner tubes. Guests may not bring in their own tubes, rafts, or ice coolers.

Borden Ice Cream Manufacturing Plant

4494 Campbell Road
Houston 77041
713-744-3700
Hours: Flexible hours, Mon.–Thurs. (call for times).
Admission free.
How to get there: Located in Spring Branch between U.S. Highway 290 and Interstate 10, off Clay Road.

The ice cream lovers in your family will feel right at home in the Borden Ice Cream Plant, which makes enough of the heavenly delight in a year to fill the Astrodome. An animated "Elsie and Elmer" begin the tour with some great stories about Gale Borden, the company's founder. You'll discover that this man not only helped draft the Texas Con-

stitution but also claims to have invented pasteurization before Louis Pasteur.

After the show, you'll walk along a glassed-in observation deck where you'll observe ten refrigerated storage tanks holding 33,000 gallons of ice cream, novelty machines making popsicles at 36,000 bars per hour, and thousands of gallons of semi-frozen ice cream squirting into spinning containers.

Don't worry. Guests get to sample one of the variety of frozen products Borden makes, from ice cream sandwiches to pudding bars to your favorite of 97 flavors.

The Police Museum

17000 Aldine-Westfield Rd.
Houston 77073
713-230-2300
Hours: 8 a.m.–3:30 p.m., Mon.–Fri.; 12 p.m.–5 p.m. Sun.
Admission free.
How to get there: Go north on Interstate 45. Exit Rankin Road and travel 4 miles to Aldine-Westfield Road. The police academy and the museum are on the corner.

Officer Danny Hare is an enthusiastic tour guide at the Houston Police Museum, and young students especially like the chance to sit behind the wheel of a real police car.

In the mid 1920s Houston Detective Owen Fondren was in a firey shoot-out with a highjacker when he caught a near-fatal bullet that came dangerously close to his spine. What saved him was a little bit of luck and his pocketwatch that deflected the bullet and death itself. Visitors to the Police Museum can examine that watch and the fateful bullet as well as a shocking collection of homemade weapons, many taken from motorcycle enthusiasts with questionable reputations. You'll also see polygraph machines and an extensive display of police uniforms from all over the world. The best exhibit, however, is the real police car complete with siren in hot pursuit of a suspect—on video.

Kids actually have a chance to sit behind the wheel as they participate in the simulated high speed chase. And, overhead hangs a real, honest-to-goodness, police helicopter.

One of the most valuable displays is a collection of guns, some real and some toy. By trying to determine which are the actual weapons, children learn that it's difficult to differentiate between what's real and what isn't. At this museum, however, they can also become more informed by studying the upstairs display of controlled substances and the related paraphernalia.

You'll leave the Police Museum having a renewed respect for the law enforcement profession, particularly if you spend a little time at "Last Roll Call," a moving tribute to those Houston officers who have lost their lives in the line of duty.

I hope you'll have an opportunity to meet Officer Danny Hare, the museum director who orchestrated the museum's opening and who now maintains it with wonderful enthusiasm. In his zany, animated fashion, he gives tours to groups of schoolkids, but his schedule is always booked two to three months in advance. If, however, you know ahead of time that you're going to be in Houston, give him a call. Located at the police academy, the museum is about 35 minutes from downtown, so go during non-peak traffic hours.

The Port of Houston

Gate 8
P.O. Box 2562
Houston 77252-2562
713-225-4044
Hours: 10 a.m. and 2:30 p.m., Tues. through Sat.; 2:30 p.m., Sun. and Thurs.
Admission free.
How to get there: Take the 610 East Loop from Houston and exit Clinton, which veers to the right. Enter the port at Gate 8.

With its 43 wharves and a record 4 million tons in imports in 1986, the Port of Houston is the third largest port in the nation. See how it all works by catching the *Sam Houston*, a "spit'n polish" vessel run by the Port Authority that gives free rides along the channel. It moors at Constitution Bend, Houston's famous ship-turning basin that has a place in Texas history books. The story goes that this bend was

See Houston's busy ship channel, the nation's third largest port, via the **Sam Houston***, the Port Authority's "spit 'n polish" cruiser.*

Photo courtesy of the Port of Houston Authority

named after the first steamboat that turned around here in June of 1837.

Brothers John and Augustus Allen were first-class promoters convinced that Buffalo Bayou would make a dandy port, although it was 50 miles from the Gulf of Mexico. So, they paid the captain of the *Constitution* $1,000 to make the trip down the bayou to Houston to prove that the port was a maneuverable water.

The trip was not easy. Lines had to be run from the trading vessel to trees and the boat had to be hauled forward by windlass. It ran aground twice and to exit the boat had to back down the narrow bayou until she reached a spot wide enough to turn around—a place now called Constitution Bend.

The *Sam Houston* won't have that much trouble. In fact, you'll enjoy the fast-paced clip of the cruiser as it passes ship after ship, most flying a foreign flag. You'll see for yourself how Houston's port affects about one third of the city's economy and generates 160,000 jobs for Texans.

So, take the trip. You'll have all the comforts of home, including an air-conditioned cabin with large glass windows for clear visibility if you don't want to sit on the deck. There are restrooms below, and on the way back, the Port Authority will spring for a soft drink for each passenger.

(Note: If you want to eat at the port, try Shanghai Red's. The captain will point it out to you in his commentary. The food is very good, and kids will enjoy the colorful atmosphere.)

The Orange Show

2401 Munger Street
Houston 77219
713-552-1767
Hours: 12 p.m.–5 p.m., Sat., Sun., and selected holidays.
Admission charged.
How to get there: Located just off the Gulf Freeway at Telephone Road.

If you happen to be off the Gulf Freeway and have always had a fetish for oranges, then by all means, visit the Orange Show. It's a . . . well, uh . . . I'll resort to the brochure . . . it's "one man's monument to the fruit he loved most." Although creator Jeff McKissack is no longer here to share his enthusiasm for life with us, his mosaic messages are still with us, embedded in the walls of the Orange Show.

It's hard to describe the Orange Show, so I'll simply say that this montage of wheels, birds, farm equipment, sculptures, gates and railings is one man's private dream and guaranteed to amaze visitors of all ages. The Orange Show is considered a "folk art environment" in some art circles, reflection of an artist's own philosophy. In McKissack's case, it's "Love the orange, and it will, in turn, keep you healthy and wise."

Whatever your feelings about the Orange Show, you'll go away having a kind of peculiar respect for Jeff McKissack, a

man with a vision. (See *Amazing Texas Monuments & Museums*, Lone Star Books, Houston, 1984.) And, who knows? You may find yourself eating more oranges.

The Lyndon B. Johnson Space Center (NASA)

Houston 77058
713-483-0123
Hours: 9 a.m.–4 p.m., daily.
Admission free.
How to get there: Take I-45 south to the NASA/Alvin exit, then go east approximately 3 miles on NASA Road 1 to the JSC visitor entrance gate on the left.

You can't possibly visit Houston without touring NASA, the birthplace of space history that is still in the making. Be prepared, though, to be a little overwhelmed at the size of the Johnson Space Center which houses the National Aeronautics and Space Administration. Like the Smithsonian Institute but on a smaller scale, visitors at NASA must walk or drive to more than one building to see everything. I suggest that you write NASA first and ask them to send you a packet of information along with a map of the center that gives you all the particulars. This way you and your family can decide what needs to be covered to pacify all in your group as well as decide how much time will be needed to see it. By contacting NASA first, they may send your child color photos of the astronauts, who are heroes at our house.

The most important thing to remember is to get there early. Although the visitor center opens at 10 a.m., be there at 9:30 a.m. This will give you time to get a good look at the huge rockets in the rocket park to the left as you enter. Park in the lot and plan to spend about 20 minutes there. "May the Force be with you" if you can understand the technical explanations posted in front of each vehicle and in turn intelligently pass your knowledge on to your children.

At a little before 10 a.m., drive over to the visitor's center, and park in front of Building 2. This building houses the most interesting and informative displays that are suited for all ages. If you want to see Mission Control, walk (or run if it's the summer and particularly Saturday morning) to the other end of the center where Gordon Cooper's *Mercury* capsule is on display. The person at the information desk will give you tickets to the 30-minute guided tour to Mission Control as well as a map that shows other visitor centers. Unless you get your tickets early, you may have to wait a half day in order to see where the Flight Director and his staff monitor space shuttle flights. Very young, wiggly children may not sit still for this tour. The kids will enjoy the exhibit hall packed with flight memorabilia, packaged space food, paintings, photos, a moon rock, and a *Gemini* Ejection Couch that the kids can really sit on. (This is a great picture spot.) Along with the *Mercury* capsule, you'll

Future scientists delight at the display of authentic space suits worn by past and present astronauts.

see the *Apollo 17* Command Module and all the astronaut suits from the first mission to the present. There are even space helmets that kids can try on.

Once you've seen Mission Control, it'll be time for lunch. You can either eat at the NASA cafeteria or pack your own. After you eat, walk over to Skylab Trainers Building (5) which is just behind the cafeteria, or you may opt for the Space shuttle Orbiter Training Building (9A) and the Lunar Sample Building (31A), both are located quite a way from Mission Control. I suggest you drive to those locations, so that once you've seen them, you can leave NASA.

Above all wear comfortable shoes and read through your packet first, so you can make the family trip to NASA a meaningful one.

Armand Bayou Nature Center

8600 Bay Area Boulevard
P.O. Box 58828
Houston 77258
713-474-2551
Hours: 9 a.m.–5 p.m., daily, except holidays.
Admission free.
How to get there: Take Interstate 45 south toward Galveston and exit
  Bay Area Boulevard. The Center is just past Bay Area Park.

Armand Bayou Nature Center, considered one of Houston's great natural treasures, is an 1,800-acre tract of wilderness that surrounds Armand Bayou, a natural estuary. According to naturalists, an estuary is a nursery ground for

shrimp, crabs, flounder, menhaden, mullet, and other sea life important to the fishing industry. Upon reaching adult size, animals born here migrate to the Gulf of Mexico. Such places, which have escaped the ravishes of the human hand, are few, yet this one is only a short distance from the Johnson Space Center.

The Center has three major ecosystems: the hardwood forest, the tall grass prairie, and the estuarine bayou. Walkways take you to the interpretive building where you can get literature about self-guided hikes, programs on canoeing, marine biology, ecology, birding, natural history, and special events that often occur at the Center.

There are strict rules here, however. No pets, picnicking, jogging, running, biking, or radios are permitted on the trails, and children under 12 must be accompanied by an adult. Most important, the gates lock at 5 p.m. so watch the time unless you plan to spend the night with the alligators.

Clear Lake Park and the *Clear Lake Queen*

3105 NASA Rd. 1; Dock 3105
Seabrook 77586
713-334-1515
Hours: Noon and 2 p.m. (excursion rides).
Admission charged.
How to get there: Take Interstate 45, then turn left on NASA Road 1.
  Go past the space center. Clear Lake Park and the Queen are two
  miles east of the Hilton Hotel.

Clear Lake Park is a beautiful old park that overlooks the lake. A pavilion only a few steps from the water offers a scenic place to have a picnic and feel the cool breezes off Clear Lake. The only problem may be the ducks and geese who also like people food. After lunch, the kids can run and play on the playground equipment while you rest a spell. One of the added features about this park, which once was the stomping grounds for the seven- and eight-foot-tall Karankawa Indians, is that it has a soft drink machine, with drinks that are ice cold. For this trip, as in the case with any outing to the park, I suggest you have a damp cloth along to wipe off the dust from knees and faces. You'll want the little Indians presentable for their ride on the *Clear Lake Queen*, docked so close by you won't even have to move the car.

If you board the vessel about 20 minutes before the 2 p.m. departure, no reservations are required. The *Clear Lake Queen*, built especially for Clear Lake, is one of the few true paddlewheelers in which the paddles actually propel the riverboat. Her design was adopted from old plans drawn by Iowa's Dubuque Boiler Works, one of America's premier riverboat builders. The 1½ hour excursion will take you in and around Clear Lake with Captain Paul Hodge or Captain Paul Beaty giving a running commentary of Clear Lake's past and present. You'll see egrets, learn about spawning of sea trout, and hear about the Karanka-was, the only true cannibals in North America. You'll also see over 8,000 slips full of sailboats, fishing boats, and yachts and will learn about some of the better restaurants on the lake.

Encourage your kids to take a seat under the boat's protected deck rather than sit out on the coverless deck in the hot sun. Soft drinks are served on board, but you may want to bring along a snack. Dinner Jazz/Blues dance cruises are offered on Saturday nights and boarding time for the Sunday night dinner cruise (adult prices run about $27) is 5:30 p.m. Children are half price.

San Jacinto Battleground State Historical Park

3800 Park Road 1836
La Porte 77571
713-479-2421
Hours: 10 a.m.–6 p.m., daily.
Admission free to monument. Admission charged to ride to the top
* (adults $2, children $.50).*
How to get there: Located just north of La Porte, 22 miles east of
* downtown Houston. Go Interstate 45 south to Interstate 610 east.*
* Take the exit at State Highway 225 east to State Highway 134. The*
* park is 3 miles on the right.*

A former governor of Tennessee, Sam Houston was an officer in the War of 1812 and a friend of President Andrew Jackson. Yet, in the face of impending battle with Santa Anna, Houston commanded his troops to turn tail and run.

Most historians believe that the "Raven," as his Indian blood brothers called him, knew that all would be lost including the newly formed Republic if he met early on with defeat. So the general stalled by leading his grumbling forces to San Jacinto where geography would be on his side. The rest is history. Houston's army of 800 ill-disciplined, volunteer Texans waited until the Mexicans were taking their afternoon siesta and then charged the sleeping troops. Of the 1,360 well-trained, well-equipped enemy, the Texans killed 630 of Santa Anna's men and captured 730 others, taking Santa Anna prisoner in the process and winning freedom for Texas.

The monument, which commemorates the sight of the battle, has in its base a museum full of more than 100,000 artifacts. Reaching skyward some 570 feet and taller than the Washington Monument, the structure is quite a sight to behold and may cause a stir even in the most complacent teenager. The limestone shaft, which was rejuvenated for the Texas Sesquicentennial, is topped with a magnificent 220-ton concrete star that is 34 feet wide as well as high. For a small fee you can take a 40-second elevator ride up to the top for a view of the battleground, the ship channel, the nearby Battleship *Texas*, and downtown Houston, 20 miles away.

There's a gift shop on the ground floor, and picnic tables around the park provide a peaceful setting for lunch.

Battleship *Texas*

713-479-2411
Hours: 10 a.m.–6 p.m., daily, May–August, 10 a.m.–5 p.m., daily,
* Sept.–April.*
Admission charged.

The *U.S.S. Texas* is moored in the San Jacinto State Historical Park and is open to visitors. Called the "last of the Dreadnoughts," she is the only surviving naval vessel to have seen service in both World Wars. Once her duty was done, she was put out to the scrapyards and would still be forgotten there today if it had not been for the state of Texas. It saved its namesake and paved the way for other states, such as North Carolina, Alabama, and Massachusetts, to do the same.

Be sure as you pay your fee to pick up a brochure that charts a self-guided tour of the vessel. It's very easy to lose your bearings once you're aboard. Also, be sure to wear tennis shoes, and I wouldn't recommend trying to carry a baby up and down those steep naval vessel ladders.

Time has not been kind to the battleship and the Texas Parks and Wildlife Department has mounted a campaign to raise the millions of dollars needed to save this historic ship.

Livingston

Alabama-Coushatta Indian Reservation

Route 3, Box 640
Livingston 77351
409-563-4391
Hours: 10 a.m.–8 p.m. summers.
Admission charged.
How to get there: 85 miles north of Houston on U.S. Highway 190
between Livingston and Woodville.

A trip through the Alabama-Coushatta Indian Reservation will give your family some understanding of life as it exists on one of two Indian reservations in Texas. Composed of 4,600 acres of the Big Thicket, the land was given to the tribes by Sam Houston soon after Texas became a Republic. Today, 550 Indians, headed by Chief Fulton Battise, live inside its boundaries which is open to tourists every day during the summer months.

Though the tribe no longer produces their lavish evening show *Beyond Sundown*, they still perform colorful tribal dances in full ceremonial dress. Some costumes are valued at as much as $5,000. War dances, the buffalo dance, and particularly the hoop dance reflect tribal history and customs. Years ago tribal dances ceased only when the campfires were totally extinguished. Caution your kids, however, to stay off the dance area before the show. The soil in the area is considered sacred ground, blessed to keep out evil spirits.

Other exhibits within the village stockade include demonstrations on long-leaf pine needle basket weaving, weaponry, and Indian cookery. Also available are two mini-tours by bus. I suggest you skip the first that takes you through the reservation, but I recommend the second, which takes tourists through the Big Thicket. The guides, all tribesmen,

Young Alabama-Coushatta Indians demonstrate ancient tribal dances on ground blessed to keep out evil spirits.

will point out such delights as a 130-foot-tall state champion water hickory, giant magnolias, swamp chestnut trees and wild oranges and elderberries. You'll find that the Big Thicket is a magnificent woodland, encompassing some 300,000 acres, where there are unique and rare varieties of life forms not found anywhere else in Texas. Dogwoods bloom here in late March and early April so you may want to plan your trip then.

Write them for their rather complex seasonal schedule, though in the summer, tours and dances take place Monday through Friday from 10 a.m. to 6 p.m. and on Sunday afternoons from 12:30 p.m. to 6 p.m.

Lufkin

Texas Forestry Museum

Texas Highway 103 East (Atkinson Dr.)
P.O. Box 1488
Lufkin 75901
409-632-TREE
Hours: 1 p.m.–4 p.m., Mon.–Sat. afternoons only.
Admission free.
How to get there: From Rusk, go south on U.S. Highway 69, which changes to Lufkin's Kurth Drive. Turn left on Timberland and right on Atkinson Drive.

On first glance, Lufkin, located in central East Texas, may not conjur up a burst of wild applause from your travel mates. However, this little lumber town has a great attraction that should be included on your Piney Woods trip agenda—the Texas Forestry Museum, operated by the state forestry association. You'll agree this certainly isn't your "run-of-the-mill" museum.

For the kids, the main attraction here will probably be the old Cyclone Hill Tower, an authentic fire lookout ranger station that's a "hands-on" exhibit in the best sense of the phrase. Children can climb into the tower, hear an actual report of the last fire reported from the station, and study maps showing the topography of Cyclone Hill. This one, typical of all these watch towers, topped long-leaf pines at 120 feet.

Other exhibits include a "talking tree," a collection of arrowheads, a cross section of a 120-year-old pine and a monstrous working steam engine performs at the press of a button. Outside the museum, the depot once used in Camden, serves as an appropriate setting for a complete vintage logging train, including steam locomotive, steam loader, and logging car.

If you're lucky, the senior citizen volunteers will be there when you visit. Some are retired timbermen who can answer even the most inquisitive (sometimes the most illogical) question from your kids. Though the museum is open afternoons only, call if you are only going to be in Lufkin in the morning. You may be able to join a visiting group as they tour this wonderful museum.

The Ellen Trout Zoo

North Loop 287 on Lufkin's north side
P.O. Drawer 190
Lufkin 75901-0190
409-634-6313
Hours: 9 a.m.–6 p.m., summers; 9 a.m.–5 p.m., winters.
Admission free.
How to get there: From Rusk, go U.S. Highway 69, then east on Loop 287. The zoo is to your left.

The Ellen Trout Zoo is not your ordinary zoo, even down to its inception. Operated by the City of Lufkin, it was founded in the 1960s when Lufkin industrialist Walter W. Trout received a hippopotamus as a Christmas gift. Today, the zoo, with 12 percent of its entire collection on the U.S. endangered species list, houses such rarities as the West African crowned crane, a bald eagle, African bushbabies, clouded leopards, and the Louisiana pine snake. Apparently the animals are happy here on this ten-acre-parcel of East Texas forestland because the zoo has the most successful reproduction rate among rare animals in the nation.

The setting is shady and serene which creates a pleasant visit, but most importantly, you're in close range of the animals who all have their own unique personalities. In fact, my little boy stood eye to eye with an ostrich who followed him as he walked back and forth in front of his cage. And, if you time it right, you'll hear a pack of timber wolves sing along with the lonesome wail of a passing train. While we were there, one of the Siberian tigers became irritated at a tourist and let out a furious growl that drew kids from all over the zoo.

If you plan to be here at lunch, bring your own because the concession only sells drinks. There's an abundance of places to picnic, however, on zoo grounds, and the kids will enjoy riding the park miniature train that offers a scenic ride around the lake.

I'm sure you'll agree once you've visited the Ellen Trout Zoo that it's definitely a winner.

Orange

If no one in your family is afraid of heights, give the kids a thrill by driving over the Rainbow Bridge, the tallest bridge in the South over a navigable stream. Arching over the Neches River on Texas Highway 87 East between Port Arthur and Orange, the 5.7-mile-long (including approaches), 177-feet-above-water-level bridge was constructed in 1927. Longtime residents say that the structure was built that tall to accommodate dirigibles (we know them as blimps) that were tied to barges, and pulled up the Neches River during the twenties and thirties.

Stark Museum of Art

712 Green Avenue
Orange 77630
Hours: 10 a.m.–5 p.m., Wed.–Sat., 1 p.m.–5 p.m., Sun. (Closed
*   Mon. and Tues.)*
Admission free.
How to get there: Exit Macarthur Dr. (Green Avenue) from U.S.
*   Highway 87.*

This amazing collection, compiled over the years by one of Orange's first families, Miriam and William Stark and philanthropist son, H. J. Lutcher Stark, comprises a virtual study in western American art. The museum takes up a full city block with 15,000 square feet of exhibition space. You'll find everything here from works by artist-naturalist John J. Audubon to sculptures by Remington and Russell, to examples of Plains Indians' body ornaments, beadwork, and clothing. Across the street is the Stark House, a magnificent 1894 Victorian mansion furnished with priceless antiques.

Take the children to this fine museum. My little boy loved it because it's full of cowboys and Indians. However, only children 14 years old or more are allowed to join a Stark House tour. (Reservations requested—call 409-883-0871.)

For a study in contrast, go to Farmer's Mercantile on the corner of 6th and Division Streets. Founded over 50 years ago, every item that was for sale in 1928 is still for sale on the shelves or in the deep bins.

Port Arthur

If you're hungry for some good seafood gumbo or a double stuffed crab, "get on down" to Port Arthur and "Laissez le bon temps roule!" or "let the good times roll!" This is Cajun land where the Cotton-Eyed Joe and the Fais-Do-Do have met on mutual ground. Try the Waterfront restaurant on U.S. Highway 73 east of Taylor's Bayou Bridge or Eellee's 4748 Main in nearby Groves. After you've had your meal, ride down to Seawall Boulevard, which borders the intracoastal canal. As ships and barges go by on a regular basis en route to and from the wharves, this will give the kids a rare chance to literally holler hello to the seamen as they work on deck of their tankers.

Notice also the three recently restored homes, which at one time belonged to prominent citizens of Port Arthur along the Boulevard. White Haven, 2545 Lakeshore, and the Vuylsteke Home, 1831 Lakeshore, can be toured by appointment. The Pompeiian Villa is usually manned by a do-

cent, but it would be better to call first. If you're a history buff, stop by Gates Memorial Library which houses the Port Arthur Historical Museum.

Pleasure Island

Pleasure Island Commission
520 Pleasure Pier Blvd.
Port Arthur 77640

Port Arthur is known as best along the Gulf Coast for its salt-water fishing, crabbing, and sailing waters. Across the channel is Pleasure Island, a 3,500-acre island which overlooks Lake Sabine, the largest saltwater lake in East Texas with 100 square miles of unobstructed water flowing into the Gulf of Mexico. Pleasure Pier, four long concrete barriers, gives anglers a more than fighting chance to catch flounder, speckled trout, croaker, drum, sheepshead, redfish, whiting, gafftop, sandtrout, and blue crab. As for sailing, it's a year-round sport on Lake Sabine (a somewhat shallow lake at 5 to 8 feet) with rental slips available in the 412-slip full service marina. Avid sailors, many of whom come from Houston and Dallas, claim the conditions here are great for sailing because there is little commercial shipping and private traffic. Dockage fees are also very reasonable.

For places to hunt and a listing of restaurants and night spots, stop by the convention and visitors bureau and ask for their comprehensive brochure, which also lists airboat tours of the bayou and festivals such as the Cajun Crawfish Festival in May.

Sailors and anglers find Port Arthur's Pleasure Island a traffic-free passageway to Lake Sabine.

Romayor

Chain-O-Lakes

P.O. Box 218
Romayor 77368
713-592-2150 or 713-592-7705
Admission charged.
How to get there: Located 18 miles east of Cleveland, between FM 787 and State Highway 146 on Daniel Ranch Road.

Chain-O-Lakes, the hidden treasure of East Texas, has everything except the dancing bears and juggling acts, and I'm sure that if you really wanted them, owners Jimmy and Beverly Smith would try to accommodate you. This 300-acre resort, dotted with thirteen spring-fed lakes, is the answer to every haggard parent's dream. Adults can sip their coffee in peace on the front porch swing of a luxurious log cabin while the children ride horses, frolic in one of the two swimming lakes, or take a hike.

Or you can relax with a fishing pole on the lake shore while bass, catfish, perch, and coppernose blue gills fight for your bait. Jimmy, a dentist from Humble who spent much of his childhood here when the resort was a simple fish camp, has sacrificed a small fortune to stock the 130 acres of lakes.

Both small children and teenagers can ride one of the twenty-four horses in residence. Gayla Clarke, the trail boss and experienced mother herself, knows horses and kids and exercises the utmost of caution.

Chain-O-Lakes, an East Texas hidden treasure dotted with thirteen spring-fed lakes, offers the family country serenity.

If horseback riding is not your saddlebag, rent a surrey or a golf cart and take a drive to the 13,000 square foot lodge, complete with game room, stage, and dance hall, where the Smiths are always cooking up some creative kind of fun. In the past, they've officiated watermelon seed-spitting contests and have even given fishing clinics for kids. They only ask that there be no motorcycle or moped riding or even gasoline motors on the lakes, for that matter. They also ask that there be no public consumption of alcohol.

Accommodations vary from luxurious "bed and breakfast" one and two bedroom log cabins, to older, more rustic camps to more primitive cabanas. If you have a camper, there are partial and full RV hookup sites and for those who like to sleep under the stars, wilderness spots (some located on private peninsulas) can be requested. My choice, however, are the country-decorated log cabins, each with a wood-burning fireplace and a loft that is a favorite of the kids. Each log cabin sits on its own lake with decks so close to the water you can hear the fish jump. The "pièce de résistance," however, is that when you stay in a cabin, you are entitled to the best breakfast you've ever put in your mouth and you don't even have to drive or walk to the Hill-

top Country Inn Restaurant, located on the grounds. Wayne Jenkel or Ned Fratangelo, owners of Classic Carriage and dressed in period "dandy," will come to your door at whatever time you desire to take you in a horse-driven carriage and deliver you and your delighted family to Mrs. Hill's door.

Known for her Hilltop Herb Farm in Cleveland, the talented Mrs. Hill conjurs up secret culinary wonders, all made from scratch and with spices that allow for salt and fat reduction.

Before you leave the restaurant, however, be sure to go out on the deck which overlooks the turtle-filled Turtle Lake and say hello to "The Governor." He's the resident alligator who'll swim up to the deck if you clap your hands.

The restaurant is open for breakfast, lunch, and dinner, with some variation according to the season. Even if you don't want to partake of the Chain-O-Lakes Resort, you can still eat at the Hilltop Country Inn Restaurant. (For information on the restaurant, call 713-592-5859.)

Rusk

Texas State Railroad

P.O. Box 39
Rusk 75785
214-683-2561
Toll free (Texas only): 1-800-442-8951
Hours: Trains depart 11 a.m. and 1:30 p.m., Thurs.–Mon. Admission charged.
How to get there: From Houston, take U.S. Highway 59 north to Lufkin and then U.S. Highway 69 north to Rusk. From Dallas, go U.S. Highway 175, then U.S. Highway 84 to Rusk.

Rusk, a quiet East Texas hamlet shares with its neighbor, Palestine, one of the state's most historic tourist attractions—the Texas State Railroad. This vintage train takes passengers down long steel ribbons that cut through the Piney Woods and pastureland that once only belonged to the Indians.

You can catch the train at either the Rusk or Palestine depot. In either place the scene is so authentic you'll feel like you're in a movie take for a western.

It's a slow pace at 1½ hours one way, but the train is fun, and you'll have to commend the Texas Parks and Wildlife

Commission for taking on the monumental task in 1976 of resurrecting the train system. Originally built in 1896 by convict labor to haul iron ore from mines to smelters and a foundry at Rusk, the line has not been used for decades. Today, however, four veteran steam engines power authentic red, black, and gold Victorian-styled cars between Rusk and Palestine through Rusk-Palestine State Park, Texas' longest and narrowest state park.

So sit back and relax. The kids will love it when the train crosses a scary 1,100-foot bridge, built in 1909, that spans the Neches River, and you'll enjoy the beautiful scenery and restful pace.

Though you can go any season other than winter, I hope you make it here in the spring when the white-blossomed dogwoods, redbuds, wild plum, and honeysuckle are in bloom. If you can't make it then, try the fall when leaves from the hardwood trees are changing to orange and gold.

But whatever time you go, arrive at the depot at least thirty minutes early. This will give kids a chance to visit with the engineer and the fireman in the engine cab. They'll learn all about the 137-ton engine but be sure the little pioneers wear tennis shoes because the boilers heat up the cab to a blistering 114 degrees and burned toes make for a miserable vacation.

Photo courtesy of the Texas State Railroad State Historical Park

Antique trains, resurrected by the Texas State Railroad, take passengers through the lush Piney Woods between Rusk and Palestine.

With the three-hour round trip, you'll have an hour for lunch, just enough time to grab a sandwich and a drink at the depot deli, or if you don't want to wait in line, you can pack your own. If you must have park food, place your order with a concession worker in the combine car as soon as the train pulls out of the station. This way, your food will be waiting for you when you deboard. The child who eats at the blink of an eye can be comforted in the fact that the combine car sells candy, ice cream and soft drinks.

One really important thing—let the weather dictate your dress because there's no air-conditioning to save you from the Texas heat. I suggest that if you go in the summer, sit on the cars with the large cut-out windows to allow maximum breeze.

The train schedule is complicated so call for times. Make reservations at least one month in advance, although on occasion you can pick up day-of-trip tickets if your group is small.

Sabine Pass

Sea Rim Park

P.O. Box 1066
Sabine Pass 77655
409-971-2559
Hours: Gates close at 10 p.m.
Admission charged.
How to get there: Head southwest along the Bolivar Peninsula on State U.S. Highway 87. The park is 12 miles from Sabine Pass.

Sea Rim Park is 15,000 acres of coastal marshland and 5½ miles of beach. A bird lover's paradise in the spring, this state facility provides the urban-weary tourist quiet seclusion from the rest of the world.

The facility has 20 RV hookups and a bathhouse with showers, and primitive camping is also allowed on the beach. Be sure the kids climb on the observation deck and venture into the museum on the second floor. They will learn all about egrets, spoonbills, alligators, sea turtles, and the red-tail hawk, just to name a few of the animals that live there. Your family will leave knowing much more about the Gulf waters, home of over 400 species of fish. On the grounds, hike down the Gambusia Nature Trail, a 7/10 mile boardwalk into the marsh. An alligator lives near the path who likes junk food so don't go in eating a hamburger or hot dog.

Woodville

Heritage Garden Village

P.O. Box 666
Woodville 75979
409-283-2272
Admission charged.
How to get there: Located 2 miles west of Woodville on U.S. Highway 190.

Why not take your family on a ride deep into the Big Thicket to Woodville where there is the curious Heritage Garden Village, the manifestation of one man's dream. This little 18th-century town, composed of some 30 buildings, is billed by creator and artist, Clyde Gray, as the "only see and touch museum town in America." Furnished with dust-coated antiques and memorabilia from a bygone era when Wyatt Earp was a household name, the village has everything from a doctor's office to a fire station to a chair factory. The pawn shop, guarded by a carved wooden Indian, is a stone's throw from an actual post office "plucked" from Pluck, Texas.

The great part about this place is there's no anxious curator following your kids around worried that they're going to break something. Guests are encouraged to examine what they find interesting.

Heritage Garden Museum is indeed an honest-to-goodness ghost town, and if you stick around long enough, you may just see some long gone resident or two hiding in the shadows.

The Pickett House

P.O. Box 856
Woodville 75979
409-283-3946
How to get there: One mile west from Woodville on U.S. Highway 190, next to Heritage Garden Village.

If you're in the mood for the kind of home cooking kids like, plan to lunch at the Pickett House, adjacent to Heritage Garden Village. The restaurant, once a 1906 schoolhouse, is set up boarding-house style with everything from chicken and dumplings, fresh okra to sassafras tea and spiced apples. If all your child will eat is fried chicken, never fear, because they serve that, too, along with stone ground corn muffins and homemade butter. All the vegetables, down to the last lima bean, are fresh and grown locally. You'll also be able to buy local syrup, honey, and freshly ground corn meal.

Don't be offended when you're required to take your empty plate and eating utensils to the kitchen. This custom of the old days will give you a chance to tell the cook how good her food is. Your family will be comfortable here, and the children will enjoy reading all the old circus posters that line the walls. Ask about the special prices for children.

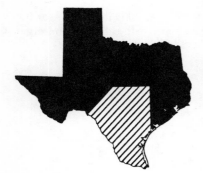

SOUTH

Burnet

Fredricksburg Johnson City **Austin**

Luckenbach Stonewall

Kerrville • Wimberley

Bandera • Boerne • New Braunfels

Vanderpool

San Antonio

Rockport

Aransas Pass

Corpus Christi • Port Aransas

Kingsville •

Laredo

Roma Los

Ebanos Pharr Harlingen

Alamo

Reynosa Port Isabel

Matamoros • Brownsville

Aransas Pass/Port Aransas

Port Aransas Chamber of Commerce
P.O. Box 356
Port Aransas 78373
512-749-5919

Aransas Pass is named for the wide channel north of Mustang Island where seafaring Spaniards entered to explore Texas' coasts. Because of its huge shrimping fleets, Aransas Pass is known today as the "shrimp capital of Texas."

Across the bay on Mustang Island is Port Aransas. It used to be a getaway for tourists weary of the crowds of other Gulf coastal resorts. Development and thousands of summer tourists have changed all that, but Port Aransas is still relatively quiet and peaceful.

While swimming and beachcombing have its rewards, Port Aransas is most famous for its fishing. Chartered fishing tours of all sorts are available. If you just want to watch, a glass-enclosed air-conditioned patio at **Fisherman's Wharf** on Station Street offers a view of fishermen bringing in their catch. From Memorial Day weekend through Labor Day, narrated sunset boat rides are available from 7:30 p.m.–9:30 p.m. **Ferry boat rides** across the ship channel are fun and free. Operated by the Texas Department of Highways and Public Transportation, the ferry runs 24 hours a day and takes about five minutes to cross. You might see porpoises frolicking in the water.

For a close-up view of every type of marine life imaginable, check out the **UT Marine Science Institute** on Cotter Avenue. Open daily from 8 a.m. to 5 p.m., their sea aquariums are available for viewing by the public, and it's free.

In spite of the recent commercial development, quaint (and inexpensive) lodgings can still be found in Port Aransas. While certainly not elegant, historic Tarpon Inn is a good choice if you like a taste of the past. This two-story frame structure with its wide verandas started out as a soldiers' barracks during the Civil War. It burned down in 1900 but was rebuilt soon afterwards.

Mustang Island State Park

P.O. Box 326
Port Aransas 78373
512-749-5246
Admission charged.
How to get there: Located 14 miles south of Port Aransas on Park Rd 53.

The island is named after the herds of wild horses that once flourished on its nourishing grasses, undoubtedly descendants of steeds left behind by Spanish conquistadores. With some 3,500 acres of sand dunes and 5 miles of beach, beachcombing can be rewarding here, especially after high tide and early in the morning. You'll also find campsites, fishing, and a nature trail.

Aransas Wildlife Refuge

Hours: 8 a.m.–5 p.m., daily.
Admission free.
How to get there: Located on Texas Hwy 35, seven miles southeast of Austwell, beyond Rockport.

This refuge is most famous for being the winter (November to March) home of whooping cranes. These ungainly birds have been around since prehistoric times and maintain a fragile toehold just this side of extinction thanks largely to this refuge. Besides the whooping crane, you can also see alligators, raccoons, javelinas, and a multitude of bird species. Stop at the Wildlife Interpretive Center for brochures and information on trails.

Near the town of Lamar on Hwy 35, just past the Sea Gun Motel is a pink building with a white roof. Here you'll find the *Whooping Crane*, the famous vessel that takes passengers along the bay side of the Aransas Wildlife Refuge for a waterside view of the whooping crane and other rare birds. Captain Brownie Brown points out the birds and sprinkles his narrative with amusing anecdotes. Write the *Whooping Crane*, Star Route 1, Box 85, Rockport, Texas 78382 or call 512-729-2341 for schedules. Reservations are recommended and a fee is charged.

Austin

No one will ever mistake Austin for Houston or Dallas. Austin manages to be a year-round summer camp for kids and grownups. An unhurried, entertaining town with a wealth of swimming holes, parks, playgrounds, and historic treasures, Austin is a great place to explore.

State Capitol Complex

11th and Congress
Austin, 78701
512-475-3070
Free guided tours 8:15 a.m.–4:30 p.m., daily.
Hours: Capitol rotunda open 7 a.m.–9 p.m., daily.
Admission free.
How to get there: Exit 11th Street off I-35, head west six blocks to Capitol Bldg. From Loop 1 (Mopac Expwy.) exit Enfield Rd, head east, turn left on Congress. Parking available on Capitol grounds and in the 1500 block of Congress.

One of the nation's most impressive state capitols, the Texas capitol sits among a lush collection of century-old oak and pecan trees. In the spring, azaleas bloom around the complex. In summer, even on the hottest of afternoons, the front lawn invites picnicking. The pink granite building is laced in detailed woodwork, and carved oak and pine doors and window frames decorate each level. Copies of the Texas Declaration of Independence and Ordinance of Secession decorate the walls of the rotunda and adjacent halls, but it is the gold inlaid five-point star in the Capitol's dome that draws the most consistent crowds.

There is a sense of wonder at wandering past office doors announcing the Lieutenant Governor or the Speaker of the House. It is hard to resist staring at each suit and tie that hurries by on the off chance you'll recognize a face from the six o'clock news.

After you've explored a bit on your own, sign up for one of the free guided tours. Available between 8:15 and 4:30 daily, the tours begin at the visitors desk in the south foyer and take roughly 30 minutes. On a tour you're taken up to the fourth floor, and this is as close as you'll get to the capitol dome. This can be a tiring trek, so plan to relax beneath the shady umbrella of oak and pecan trees on the capitol's inviting front lawn of the capitol afterward. To the east of the Capitol is the **Archives–Library** (512-475-2619) with on-going exhibits on Texas history. The **Old Land Office Building** (512-477-1822) sits at the southeastern corner of the complex, where original documents of early settlers to Texas are on display. Stop in at the **Old Bakery and Empo-**

rium (512-477-5961) for a look at a 19th-century bakery that is now run by area senior citizens. The homemade chocolate chip cookies are a perfect compromise until dinnertime.

A Texas favorite tourist attraction is its famous Capitol. Tours are offered daily.

Zilker Park

2100 Barton Springs Rd
Austin
512-477-6511
Hours: 6 a.m.–10 p.m., daily.
Admission free. (Admission charged to Barton Springs pool.)
How to get there: Exit Rollingwood from Loop 1 (Mopac) and follow the signs to the park.

With the skyline standing guard to the north and the Hill Country stretching out to the southwest, Zilker Park is a terrific middle ground. Four hundred acres encompass Texas' finest swimming hole, Barton Springs (512-476-9044). With a year-round temperature of 69 degrees, this 1,000-foot-long, spring-fed pool is lined with shady oaks, sloping lawns, and the best-tanned bodies in Austin. Only the very brave dare to jump directly in—the water is so cold it can easily take your breath away. (Barton Springs is lined with trained lifeguards.) For sunbathing and people-watching, there is no better headquarters. Floats and other toys are allowed in the water, and there is a puddle-deep section for toddlers.

A city park since 1917, Zilker is roomy enough to accommodate a dozen soccer games at once. An 18-hole frisbee-golf course was recently set out and an improved hike-and-bike path draws out the city's running elite. The park fronts a beautiful stretch of Town Lake where paddleboats, canoes, and two-man sailboats (life jackets are provided) can be rented. For kids partial to fishing, just grab a pole and bait and pick your spot along the banks—no guarantees you'll even get a nibble, but the setting is peaceful.

When it comes time to set your children loose in a safe place while you relax for a moment, head for **Playscape** (follow park signs to the parking area). This playground is a haven for the energetic and the weary. Over-sized trucks and slides, well-planted swingsets, and manicured tree stumps for climbing are all within your field of vision from beneath covered picnic tables where parents can sit and re-group. The concession stand, bathrooms, and water fountains are nearby, as is the "depot" for the miniature train that runs every half hour through the park. (An admission is charged.)

Zilker also has its own live performance stage, Zilker Hillside Theater (information through main number, admission free). A variety of musical and theatrical productions in addition to the Austin Symphony's Fourth of July

There's nothing like a good romp in the park for all that excess energy kids store up, and Austin's Zilker Park is one of the best parks in Texas.

concert are scheduled throughout the year. If you are planning to attend a performance, be sure to take something to sit on and a bit of refreshment and get to the park about an hour before showtime.

Zilker Gardens/Austin Area Garden Center

2200 Barton Springs Rd
Austin
512-477-7341
Hours: daily until sunset.
Admission free.

Turning off Barton Springs into this heavily wooded, flower-laden refuge, it is hard to imagine what lies ahead. Acre upon acre of lush vegetation stretches out around you. There is a hush in the air that is not too often interrupted by other visitors. The pathway winds up and down until you reach the bamboo-and-stone shelter that provides a stunning view of downtown. While the setting is particularly romantic and the site of many weddings, it is also a great treat for kids. Wander around the lily ponds, the tiny waterfall, and exquisite rose garden. The **Garden Center** provides information on the Gardens as well as tidbits from the city's colorful history and most weekdays you will be virtually sole possessor of the Gardens.

Jourdan-Bachman Pioneer Farm

11418 Sprinkle Cut-Off Rd
Austin 78754
512-837-1215
Hours: Open to visitors by reservation only.
How to get there: Take the Braker Lane exit off I-35, head east. Braker will deadend into Dessau Lane, turn left. Immediately after crossing Walnut Creek, just at the top of the hill, turn right onto Sprinkle Cut-Off Rd. Look for the front gates.

"It ain't fancy, but we got a roof shading us from falling stars, a hearth big as Papa's backside, and room for you to come visit. Today I'm learning to cure sausage"—from a letter from newly settled Austin man to his maiden sister back in Abilene.

For the fertile imaginations of children, J-B Pioneer Farm recreates scenes from every John Wayne movie ever made. Aiming to portray Central Texas farm living as it was in the early 1800s, the farm is an authentic time capsule.

On 70 acres along Walnut Creek, twelve renovated buildings—with more structures from the period on the way—house a blacksmith shop, a log cabin for spinning and loomwork, al fresco kitchens cooking up candles and strong lye soaps, and an actual Indian teepee. Visitors are invited to prowl around, ask questions of the well-versed "farm hands," get a close-up look at the farm's animals, and tool through acre upon acre of field crops.

Each month there is a special program highlighting one aspect of the farming life. Pioneer skills of hide tanning, meat curing, beekeeping, sausage-stuffing, quilting, rock masonry, cooking over an open fire. Impromptu demonstrations of these skills are given continuously, and more often than not there are a few activities that children are invited to participate in. One of the all-time favorites is the feeding of the animals, when kids, under the watchful supervision of the Pioneer Farm staff, can walk right up and pet some of the larger-than-life beasts.

After all the excitement, a picnic is just the trick. In addition to your goodies, be sure to bring along a blanket to sit on—the ants in this region have laid claim to the banks of the creek and there's simply no fighting them. Kick off your sneakers for some hard-earned wading in the cool waters of Walnut Creek—this also is a skill dating back to the days of pioneering, but it still feels great.

Mayfield Park

3505 W. 35th (Old Bull Creek Rd)
512-453-7236
Hours: 8 a.m.–5 p.m., daily.
Admission free.
How to get there: Take the 35th St. exit off Loop 1 and head west. The park will be on your left. Follow the signs. Parking available.

Sans ordinary playground equipment, picnic tables, or hike-and-bike trails, kids are immediately suspicious of Mayfield Park. All question will be wiped soon enough from their faces when they catch their first glimpse of the pack of peacocks that call Mayfield home. Miles of flagstone paths weave through this quiet, dreamlike acreage. Tiny ponds filled with the heartiest of goldfish and beautiful water lilies dot the wooded park. Tame deer wait to be fed (a highly recommended snack is bread crumbs), and such community has formed between the deer and the peacocks, they have been known to grab greedily for the same handful of food.

From the entrance to the park, head back toward Loop 1 to the grounds of Camp Mabry. To your left (north) you will be able to spot the enormous collection of real-life military equipment: actual rockets, tanks, helicopters and jets. And the best part: each is ready to be climbed on and explored.

Mt. Bonnell

Crest of Mt. Bonnell Rd
Hours: 8 a.m.–10 p.m., daily.
Admission free.
How to get there: Go 1 mile beyond the west end of W. 35th on Mt. Bonnell Road

At 785 feet, this is the highest point within the city limits and the ideal place to take in Austin's expanse. The climb up the 99 quick steps affords about 89 magnificent views of the city. Be sure to stop during the ascent and look around.

You're sure to lose your kids on the stairs and the surrounding hillside; just agree that you'll all meet at the top and then relax. This can be a 25-minute aerobic challenge, or it can turn into a more in-depth study of the Texas landscape. To cover your bets, bring along a thermos of juice or a couple of soft drinks. It is well worth the extra baggage on the short climb up. Sunburns are a real possibility; pass out the visors to all sensitive skin types and enjoy.

McKinney Falls State Park

7102 Scenic Loop Road
Austin 78744
512-243-1643
Hours: Opens at 8 a.m. and park gates are locked at 9 p.m.
Admission charged for day passes and camping.
How to get there: Take U.S. Hwy 183 south to FM 812 and turn right on Scenic Loop Rd.

Even though McKinney Falls is just a heartbeat away from the city limits, hop in the car and plan a day of exploring. This portion of Onion Creek is a magnet for avid fishermen. With two sets of scenic falls and the gathering of hearty cedar and cypress trees, a days' worth of hiking can be fun. While there is no swimming, there are plenty of shallow creeks to splash around in. Maps of the park are available at the Visitor Center, and marked trails will take you through an ancient Indian campground—one of the oldest yet discovered in Central Texas. As indicated on the maps, head down to the Lower Falls where everyone can enjoy the cleaner waters of Onion Creek. Lined with enormous granite boulders, this natural wading pool is just what the kids have been waiting for since hearing the name McKinney Falls. Niagara these are not. However, they do the trick on hot summer days—and the sound of the rushing water is heavenly. Campsites, restrooms, picnic tables, and playgrounds are available, but weekends usually find the campgrounds full. Bring along bathing suits, a change of clothes and shoes if you can, towels, and enough K-rations for hungry, pooped out (possibly even grumpy) kids. Campground reservations are taken by phone in advance. (See *Camper's Guide to Texas Parks, Lakes, and Forests, 2nd Edition*, Lone Star Books, Houston, 1986.)

Lyndon B. Johnson Library

2313 Red River
Austin 78705
512-482-5136
Hours: Open daily 9 a.m.–5 p.m. Tours available for groups of 12 or more.
Admission free.
Parking on Red River between E. 26th and Manor Rd.

"We've been in there all day, but the President wasn't home."—one Austin first grader to another.

From its summit-like perch overlooking the University of Texas environs, the LBJ Library has long been recognized as one of the finest presidential libraries in the nation. This is as much due to the collection as to the larger-than-life figure LBJ was.

You will feel like a window shopper gazing at the hefty collection of extravagant gifts presented to the President by world leaders, celebrities, and ardent Johnson followers, and even small children will be entertained. The library also presents American political memorabilia dating to 1789, along with a replica of the Oval Office. Displays trace Johnson's successful political career, and they certainly don't downplay his ties to Texas. The library also houses four entire stories filled with presidential papers, all enshrined in red boxes with gold seals.

Kids have an amazing curiosity where Presidents are concerned, and the LBJ Library can be a true catalyst for young minds. Check the information number for current schedules of traveling exhibits, lectures, films, and concerts going on at the Library.

Deep Eddy/Austin Nature Center Annex

401 Deep Eddy
Austin
512-472-4523
Hours: Pool—8 a.m.–9 p.m. daily in the summer. Science Center—8
  a.m.–5 p.m., Mon.–Fri.; 9 a.m.–5 p.m., Saturday.
Admission charged.
Parking lots fill immediately. Additional parking along Deep Eddy and
  across Lake Austin Blvd.

Forever eclipsed by the reputation and renown of Barton Springs, Deep Eddy was long-ago relegated to being the little brother of Austin swimming spots. Every bit as refreshing (the water is actually lake water from nearby Town Lake), Deep Eddy is simply not as high-profile. Still, the clear, lightly chlorinated water, towering shade trees, and ample sunbathing space draw a loyal contingent. And best of all, it is rarely as crowded as Barton Springs. The pool is divided into two sections—the lap pool and the swimming section. The gaggle of alert lifeguards enforce the rules with a strict but gentle authority.

Next door to the pool is a local treasure in the Austin Nature Center. Headquarters for the Parks and Recreation Department's Outdoor Nature Programs, the Center offers classes and activities for all ages—from 18 months to 18 years—such as wildflower hikes, Ottine Swamp trips, Lost Maples camping trips, backpacking for a weekend along the Wind River. Adult classes range from "environmental eating" to beekeeping and wildlife rehabilitation.

Inside the Center, kids can take a look at exhibits of Indian artifacts, native plants and insects and end up at the tiny aviary. If you've spent a long day at the pool, count on hungry kids. While there is junk food near the pool, it makes better sense to pack a lunch of your own. There are

picnic tables in the park and bleachers near the pool where you're welcome to watch the swimmers while you eat. Be sure to bring cover-ups to pull on after swimming for the quick walk through the **Science Center.**

Hike and Bike Trail

Town Lake
How to get there: Exit 1st St. off Loop 1 heading east. Along Town
  Lake there are parking areas marked, with easy access to the trail.

Along this cleared and improved pathway is a beautiful look at Austin—both the people and the city. There are ducks demanding to be fed, paddle boats, sailboats, and canoes for rent (just north of the Hyatt Hotel waterfront), strategically placed benches to rest on, and fabulous views of downtown and Zilker Park.

Be sure to look around for identifying landmarks—Austin High School, the YMCA, downtown, or the bridges that cross over the lake for a point of reference. When hiking with kids, pay attention to the time; it is too easy to get out farther than you really want to hike back. The entire loop, the Mopac bridge to the S. 1st bridge, is 5.4 miles. There **are tenth-mile markers along the path.**

At Austin's Town Lake there are ducks to be fed, boats to be paddled, and wonderful trails to be hiked.

Hamilton Pool

512-973-9333
Hours: Use is restricted, so call ahead.
Admission charged.
How to get there: Located 25 miles west of Austin on Hamilton Pool
  Road off Hwy 71 west.

Well-protected by the surrounding countryside, Hamilton Pool has been a favorite swimming hole for a good fifty years. Named for a spring-fed pool inside a cave where an enormous waterfall provides an unlimited water supply, the pool has not changed a great deal over the years. The most significant change is the upgrade from swimming hole to county park. Use is limited to 100 cars.

Bandera

Chamber of Commerce
Bandera 78003

Welcome to the town that survived a colorful history filled with Indian raids, outlaws, and a waxing and waning shingle industry. Today Bandera is given to more civilized pursuits: horseback riding, squaredancing, dude ranches, county fairs, chili cookoffs, and four-star barbecues.

Bandera is home to one of the more entertaining restaurants in the Hill Country, the **O.S.T.** (307 Main, 512-796-3836. Open for breakfast, lunch, and dinner. Call for hours). This Tex-Mex fare is as fresh as it gets.

For the curious pack who has not yet visited the West Texas community of Langtry, make time to stop by **Roy Bean's Court** (Texas Hwy 173 at 12th) Roy Bean's "Law West of the Medina," purported to be the one-time courthouse of the colorful frontier judge, greets visitors as they enter town. The ricketty, slatted-board, one-room cabin, home of the Bandera Chamber of Commerce, is an ideal spot for a group photo on the front porch.

Dude ranches are big business out here along Texas Hwy 16. For full information on what is available, rates, seasons, etc., contact the Chamber of Commerce. For some outdoor excitement, try wading in the Medina River, guaranteed to cool off even the stickiest of days. Campgrounds north of the river provide access to the riverbanks, as do many hotels along the route.

The area's best swimming can be enjoyed at **Medina Lake.** To get there take Texas Hwy 16 south toward San Antonio. Watch for signs for FM Rd 1283 and turn right at Pipe Creek. Continue to Park Rd 37, look for signs for Medina Lake. Here is the state's oldest large-scale reservoir project. The dam across the Medina River created a lake that covers over 5,000 acres. The adjacent park offers a boat ramp, but as a private enterprise provides none of the expected facilities.

Frontier Times Museum

506 13th St
Bandera 78003
Hours: 10 a.m.–noon, 1 p.m.–4:30 p.m., Mon.–Sat., 1 p.m.–4:30
  p.m., Sun.
Admission charged.
How to get there: Go east on Pecan St. from the courthouse and follow
  the signs.

In a quick sweep through, you'll be treated to a fabulous collection of frontier oddities. Our favorites included the map of Texas done in full relief using rattlesnake rattles and the large selection of obscure books on Texas history. There are alarmingly graphic photos of dead Texas outlaws, always a big hit with the under-15 crowd.

Boerne

Cascade Caverns

Rt 4 Box 4110
Boerne 78006
512-755-8080
Hours: 9 a.m.–6 p.m., daily, April–Labor Day 9 a.m.–5 p.m., daily,
  Labor Day–March.
Admission charged.
How to get there: Exit I-10 at Cascade Caverns Rd, turn left at Boerne
  Stage Rd on to Cascade Caverns Rd and follow the signs.

From the 91° summer afternoon temperature outside, the temperature inside the caverns drops nearly 30° to a damp 65°. Named for an underground waterfall that drops nearly

100 feet from a stream high above, Cascade Caverns is an active, water-formed Texas cave. Locals knew about the cave years before it was made famous by Carlsbad Cavern researcher and explorer Frank Nicholson in late 1932. His description of the caverns included tales of all sorts of odd animal life within. The floor of the present day cave was covered by an enormous underground lake. When the water level receded, due to movement deep within the earth, the full depth of the cave was discovered. Stalagmite and stalactite formations are estimated to grow about 1 inch every 100 years. Tours take about an hour and cover about one-half mile of the caverns. There are campgrounds nearby and a recreation area for kids.

Brownsville, the Valley, and Mexico

Valley Chamber of Commerce
FM 105 and Hwy 83
Weslaco 78596
512-968-3141

Gladys Porter Zoo

Brownsville 78520
Hours: 9 a.m. to dusk, year round.
Admission charged.
How to get there: Going south on U.S. 83, take the first Brownsville exit marked for the zoo and follow the signs.

The Gladys Porter Zoo is a *must* on your tour of South Texas. It has to be one of the best zoos for small children in the country, if not *the* best. Formed concrete made to look like stone creates a natural-looking environment for the 1,800 animals who live here. The zoo is carefully landscaped and planted with unusual tropical flora, all as neatly identified as the animals themselves. The care taken in the creation of the environment ensures that children will never be distressed by sad animals peering from behind bars. The zoo is built on a resaca of the Rio Grande River, and its waterways make natural boundaries between sections. These are divided into the four geographical areas of Tropical America, Indo-Australia, Asia, and Africa. Because of its clever circular layout, all of the zoo's animals can be seen in under two hours.

The animals, many of which are endangered species, are sleek, relaxed and happy. As proof of that, their reproduction rate is prolific by zoo standards. One of the female gorillas has the most babies of any other gorilla in the country; she can usually be observed tolerating the antics of her latest youngster.

Photo courtesy of Gladys Porter Zoo

One of the most delightful features of Brownsville's Gladys Porter Zoo is its nursery. Penny, a lowland gorilla, made her debut there in November 1986.

Children will be just as delighted with the petting zoo and nearby nursery, where they can watch the baby monkeys or wallabies or bears, depending on the season.

From the pink flamingoes sitting on their earthern nests at the entrance to the zoo, to the elephants bathing their babies in the African section at the far end, the Gladys Porter Zoo is a wonderful learning experience big and little children will never forget. Several food concessions are available, and strollers and wheelchairs can be rented cheaply. On Sunday afternoons between 1:30 and 3:00, a tram makes a guided tour of the zoo.

When you have seen the zoo take your picnic across the street to the **Dean Porter Park.** It has areas for eating and a playground for the kids.

The Confederate Air Force

Industrial Air Park
Harlingen 78550
512-425-1057
9 a.m.–5 p.m., Mon.–Sat.; 1 p.m.–6 p.m., Sun.
Admission charged.
How to get there: Exit Hwy 77 north of Harlingen at the sign for the Valley International Airport. The Industrial Airpark is west of the airport.

The famous Confederate Air Force is a major attraction in the South Texas area. It was begun in the mid-fifties by a handful of men who were interested in preserving the flying machines used by both the Allies and the Axis in World War II. They began their plane collection with one aircraft, the P-40 Warhawk. As a joke, one of the men painted "Confederate Air Force" on the side of the plane, and thus coined the name for the collection. It is also known as the "Ghost Squadron." You will certainly feel a shiver down your spine as you contemplate these reminders of a war long past. Also as a sort of joke, the founders began wearing gray uniforms and calling one another "bird" colonels, the nickname for full colonels in the flying military. Today, there are some 7,000 bird colonels who have paid their $200 application fee from all parts of the world in the Confederate Air Force. The colonel fees along with admission and concession proceeds go toward maintaining the aircraft in flying condition, a considerable expense of millions of dollars per year.

The main attraction of the museum—the old planes themselves—await inspection in hangars outside the museum. Some of the aircraft are beautifully restored and in flying condition, and some are merely to look at, their flying days long over. Most of the planes inside the hangars are for your eyes only, but the planes outside on the ramp may be touched and admired close up (but not climbed on).

There's no way to know which planes will be at the air museum at any given time, since they're in demand in airshows all over the country, but you'll always find a good selection available for viewing at the CAF museum.

Displays inside the museum include World War II military uniforms, from the SS outfits of Nazi Germany to U.S.

Photo courtesy of Confederate Air Force

There's no better place for a lesson in WWII history than the Confederate Air Force in Harlingen with its fabulous collection of aircraft from "The Big One."

sailor suits. Photographs and local memorabilia, such as ration booklets, as well as guns, torpedoes, and defused bombs, are on display.

If you're lucky enough to be near South Texas in early October, don't miss the big annual CAF Airshow. The stars of the show are the restored World War II aircraft flown in from all over the world. The show lasts five or six hours out in the October sun, which in the Valley can still be quite warm. So take hats, sunscreen, and cool drinks.

While in the Industrial Airpark, stop by to look at the original model used in the casting of the famous **Iwo Jima Memorial,** depicting soldiers raising the U.S. flag over Iwo Jima in World War II.

Santa Ana National Wildlife Refuge

Rt 2 Box 202A
Alamo 78516
512-787-3079
Hours: 8 a.m.–4:30 p.m., Mon–Fri., 9 a.m.–4:30 p.m., Sat.
Admission free.
How to get there: Exit south off U.S. 83 at Alamo on Hwy 281 and follow the signs.

The Santa Ana National Wildlife Refuge provides a welcome break from the highway doldrums. All manner of creatures make their home here, including more than 50 threatened or endangered species. First, go to the center at the entrance of the refuge to browse at the exhibits. A nice prelude to hiking one of the nature trails is to watch the 30-minute slide show of native animals of the area, shown on request. The trails are conveniently marked according to how long they are and how many minutes it takes to walk them. Who knows? You or your progeny might spot one of the 11 species of amphibians, 33 reptiles (including some 18 species of snakes), and 33 mammals, including the ocelot and jaguarundi. The 355 species of birds found here make it a paradise for birdwatchers, too.

If you don't feel like hiking, you can drive through the refuge. The drive takes about 20 minutes at 20 mph. You'll pass through a shady canopy of chaparral and Texas ebony trees dripping with Spanish moss. (This might be the only place in the world where you'll see a roadsign warning motorists to stop for chachalacas crossing the road!) At several points along the road, you can park and go down a foot path. My favorite stop leads to a small cemetery. Between December and March you can also take a guided tram tour through the refuge.

Los Ebanos Ferry Crossing

Los Ebanos 78565
Hours: 9 a.m.–5 p.m., daily.
Admission charged.
How to get there: Take U.S. 83 west out of Mission for 14 miles. Turn on FM 886 to the town of Los Ebanos, then drive south to the river.

At the tiny town of Los Ebanos you'll find the only hand-pulled ferry at an international border anywhere in the world, so they say. You can tell the kids about how in olden times bandidos and cattle rustlers forded the Rio Grande at this very spot. Today, it takes two to five men to haul across the rather rickety wooden ferry, which holds two cars and a few pedestrians. The crossing takes about five minutes.

After maneuvering your car up the steep bank on the other side, you'll find a sleepy Mexican town amid fields of cotton, not to mention a long line of cars waiting to recross the river. Because of the latter, you might opt for riding the ferry as a foot passenger, or even just observing the scene from the bench under the big ebony tree on the U.S. side of the border.

Photo by Michael Murphy. Courtesy of Tourism Division, Texas Department of Commerce

Kids will love this ancient hand-drawn ferry crossing the Rio Grande at Los Ebanos.

Roma

Hwy 83

The aura of the Old West pervades this small border town. This pretty hamlet has been designated a national historic district, and fifteen blocks in it are listed in the National Register of Historic Places.

After the Civil War, prosperous merchants hired fine craftsmen to erect grand buildings. The wealth of earlier and happier days is still evident in many of these ancient edifices. On the Old Plaza, start off at **Our Lady of Refuge Catholic Church.** The church building was rebuilt after being demolished in 1962, but the original bell tower remains. Make a walking tour of the streets surrounding the plaza, especially Convent and Portcheller Streets, where nearly all of the buildings have Texas Historical Markers. At Convent and Portcheller Streets is the residence used as "Rosita's Cantina" in the filming of the movie *Viva Zapata.* Don't be surprised if you find yourself rubbing elbows with artists and photographers. The tiny **Roma Historical Museum** on Estrella Street keeps irregular hours but is worth looking into.

About 12 miles from Roma off Hwy 83 on FM 2098 is **Falcon Dam.** The construction of this dam marked the end of flooding which plagued many towns along the Rio Grande,

Roma is an old border town caught in time. You expect Pancho Villa to come galloping by at any minute.

Photo courtesy of Starr County Industrial Foundation

and the beginning of the irrigation that transformed the face of the Valley.

Mexico

Since Mexico and all things Mexican are so much a part of South Texas, your South Texas tour should include a visit to at least one border town. Border towns are great for shopping, eating at selected restaurants, and soaking up the foreign atmosphere.

For day trips into border towns, all you need is proof of U.S. citizenship. You see a lot more if you park your car on the U.S. side and walk across. When little feet start to drag, consider taking a taxi to return. Establish the fare beforehand. If you take your car across, buy Mexican car insurance first. In Mexico, people honk their horns a lot. It's a necessary part of maneuvering in traffic there, so don't hesitate to join in. It's customary to tip the man who motions you into a parking space, and also the boy (or girl) who watches your car.

Photo opportunities abound. If you want to take a photograph of a person, be sure to ask permission first and give a $1 tip.

Better to steer clear of raw vegetables and stick to bottled soft drinks or mineral water instead of tap water.

On recrossing into Texas you are allowed $300 worth of duty free merchandise.

Matamoros, Mexico

Across the border from Brownsville

This bustling city of lush tropical foliage and elegant old buildings has a population of about 350,000. Whether you decide to walk, drive, or hire a taxi to take you around, there are several interesting places to see.

The **Casa de la Cultura** (Culture Center) on Calle 5 is a contemporary building housing exhibits of artistic creation ranging from paintings to pottery. Proceed eight blocks along Calle 5 to the plaza, and explore the **Cathedral Nuestra Señora del Refugio,** founded in the year 1800. The present building dates from 1934, the original having been destroyed in a 1933 hurricane.

Two blocks beyond the plaza on Calle Morelos, turn left on Calle 13 and you'll find yourself at an old cemetery. French, English, Italian and Irish names on the tombstones are testaments to the merchants from these nations who moved to Matamoros in the early 1800s and made their fortunes in the mercantile business.

If you hire a taxi to give you a tour, be sure to mention Colonia San Francisco, a neighborhood of fine homes owned by the wealthy of Matamoros. Pass by the lovely lake in the heart of the city, too. Ask to visit **Casa Mata**, a fort and the oldest building in Matamoros. During the Mexican War Fort Mata was the site of military headquarters in Matamoros. From here a cannon was fired at General Zachary Taylor's men across the river. The fort is now a museum, open Wednesday through Monday. Admission is free.

Calle 6 and Calle Abasolo is a pedestrian mall closed to vehicular traffic and is a shopper's dream.

If you work up an appetite in Matamoros, try **Garcia's,** one of its best known restaurants. It's on the main street (Calle Obregon) after crossing the International Bridge. Keep to the right at the fork in the road and watch for it on the left. On the right near the end of the second block is **Blanca White's** restaurant, known for its traditional Mexican food. While you're in the neighborhood, drop in at Barbara's, in the middle of the next block. It's a shop featuring some of Mexico's finest artisans, housed in a charming old home. The eye-catching papier-mâché and brass sculptures of animals created by Sergio Bustamente delight all ages. (See *Traveling Texas Borders*, Lone Star Books, Houston, 1983.)

Reynosa, Mexico

Across the border from McAllen

In McAllen, take the 10th or 23rd Street exit off Hwy 83 and in a few minutes you'll be at the Mexican border town of Reynosa, a bustling city of more than 300,000 people. Just across the international bridge is the **Zona Rosa** (pink zone), where shopping spots and nightclubs abound. Try Trevino's for jewelry and unusual and well made clothing. For eating, try the **Imperial Bar,** which has a waterfall and a mariachi band, or **La Cucaracha, Sam's,** or the luxurious **La Mansion.**

Head toward the spire of the cathedral and you'll find yourself at the plaza. Walk along the west side of the plaza heading south and at the right hand corner of Hidalgo and Matamoros Streets is the **Zaragoza Market.** You can spend hours browsing here. Clothing and leather goods are good bargains.

For a guided tour of the town, you can hire a taxi at the plaza. Be sure to arrange for the fee ahead of time. Reynosa also has bullfights, but they are definitely not recommended for children.

Burnet

Fort Croghan

Burnet
Hours: 8 a.m.–5 p.m., Mon, Tues, Fri., Sat.; 1 p.m.–5 p.m., Sun.
Admission charged.
How to get there: Take Texas Hwy 29 west out of town.

For a fun stroll through some of Texas' more rambunctious history, Fort Croghan is a good sidetrip. One of a trail of frontier forts, Croghan was built in 1849 and operated at full capacity warding off Indian attacks and offering refuge to soldiers for about five years. After the fort was officially closed in 1855, it remained a meeting place for locals and some of the barracks were used as temporary housing for frontier residents of Burnet.

Walk through the Powder House, a stone building used to store ammunition, and the only building original to the

fort still standing. Four other historic stone structures from that era were moved to the site in 1957 by the Burnet County Historical Society. A sampling of late 1800s tools, furniture, military paraphernalia and a hodge podge of collectibles from families in the area now make up the Fort Croghan Museum.

Inks Lake State Park

Box 117
Buchanan Dam 78609
512-793-2223
Hours: Open all year
Admission charged.
How to get there: Take US Hwy 281 south three miles to Park Rd 4, follow signs to Inks Lake.

Take time to pull over and enjoy the scenic overlook along Park Rd 4; a hefty arm of Inks Lake. You'll be gazing out over **Devil's Waterhole.** Complete with a surprising waterfall, Devil's Waterhole offers a good look at the combination of wildflowers, cactus, and oak trees that cover the hillsides, not to mention the unmistakable hues of Texas pink granite that make up the area formation known as the Llano Uplift. Park rangers are easy to find and ready to answer questions and help with directions.

Are you ready for some unusual swimming holes? There is also water skiing, fishing, scuba diving, and boating (both paddle and motor) on the lake. Campsites in the park range from primitive with only numbered markers and open land, to the privileged with water and electrical hookups.

Longhorn Caverns State Park

Rt 2 Box 23
Burnet 78611
512-756-6976
Hours: Tours on the half hour 10 a.m.–5 p.m., daily, Memorial Day–Labor Day; tours at 10 a.m., 1 p.m., and 3 p.m., Mon.–Fri., tours on the hour 10 a.m.–5 p.m., Sat. and Sun., Sept.–May. (Closed Mon. and Tues., Oct.–Feb.)
Admission charged (group rates available).
How to get there: Take U.S. Hwy 281 south 11 miles from Inks Lake and follow the signs to the park.

With formations dating back to the Ice Age, one million years ago, Longhorn Caverns has a tumultuous history filled with raging underground rivers, receding glaciers, ferocious animals, bands of Indians, and outlaws in hiding. During the hour-and-a-half tour visitors are inundated with facts about stalactites (hanging from the ceiling), stalagmites (building from the floor), dazzling crystal and flint formations, and the grand finale, the Hall of Marble. If your kids haven't seen Carlsbad Caverns, this is a wonderful introduction to the damp, cool, mysterious underworld. Cameras and flashlights are not allowed. Be sure to wear tennis shoes as the ground tends to be uneven, dimly lit, and damp. My six-year-old companion was a bit spooked by the dark, but as soon as we could see the light of day he was fine and ready to dive into our picnic lunch. In spring, there's no passing up a picnic among the wildflowers. Nature walks and rock hounding get you acquainted with the surface geology and the caverns take on an almost science fiction quality when you can see no real evidence of their existence from the outside.

Vanishing Texas River Cruise

Burnet
512-756-6986
Hours: Call for schedules. Reservations required.
Admission charged.
How to get there: Take Texas Hwy 29 west three miles, turn right onto FM 2341 and head northwest 15 miles.

From air-conditioned cabins, you enjoy an in-depth, two-and-a-half-hour tour of the wildlife inhabiting the Hill Country, Lake Buchanan, and the Colorado River. You may see deer, rabbits, armadillos, and an occasional wild hog as well as egret, pelicans, Great Blue Herons and osprey. And from mid-November through as late as March, American Bald Eagles have been spotted. The narration along the trip is both lively and informative and kids love to hang out on the open-air observation deck—a real test for protective parents. Trust that the boat is safe, sit back, and enjoy the scenery. Depending on the time of day you depart, you might want to bring along some snacks. Sunglasses and warm-ups were great to have along on our late-March excursion. Guides can fill you in on what to expect weatherwise when you call for reservations.

Corpus Christi

Corpus Christi Convention and Tourist Bureau
P.O. Box 2664
Corpus Christi 78403
512-882-5603

Corpus Christi, the "Sparkling City by the Sea," is the biggest resort on the "Texas Riviera." This city of 260,000 offers a multitude of activities, from black-tie cultural events to just plain beach bumming. Corpus is also an important deep sea port. But as far as tourists are concerned, it's probably most important for its beautiful white sand beaches.

Corpus Christi Beach on the north side of the channel has swimming, restrooms, park areas, and picnic tables. If you get tired of swimming and sand castles, on People's

Photo courtesy of Corpus Christi Convention and Tourist Bureau

To roam the seawall at Corpus Christi, rent a fringe-topped surrey for two with a kiddie basket in front.

Street T-Head you can rent aqua cycles, jet skis, paddle boats, roller skates, sailboards for windsurfing, and sailboats. To roam the seawall, rent a fringe-topped surrey. These pedal-powered vehicles seat two adults and have a "kiddie basket" in front.

After an active day on the beach, you might be ready to relax and take a cruise of the bay. The *Gulf Clipper* is a sightseeing boat that offers one-and-a-half hour harbor and bay tours, beginning at 10:30 a.m., 1 p.m., 4:30 p.m. and 8. Call 512-882-9462. In the next slip is the *Flagship*, a triple-decker paddleship (512-643-7128 or 512-884-1693). It tours the bay and harbor, and on Saturday nights has a live band. Corpus Christi seen at night from the bay is a spectacular sight.

The pleasures of the sand and sea are only a part of what Corpus Christi has to offer the vacationer. It you like touring old homes, the **Heritage Park** section of town has several well preserved examples of Victorian architecture, all open to the public. Put on comfortable shoes and stop by the **Galvan House** to pick up the brochure "A Walking Tour of Heritage Park." The Galvan House is open from 10 a.m.–4 p.m. Monday through Friday and 10 a.m. to 2 p.m. on Saturdays.

Corpus Christi has several museums of special interest to children. The unusual **International Kite Museum** showcases—what else?—kites. It's free and open 7 days a week on the grounds of the Best Western Sandy Shore Resort. If you get hoarse in museums from repeated warnings of "Look, don't touch," then the **Corpus Christi Museum** will

be a welcome change of pace. Billed as the "museum where you can touch things," it features many exhibits that welcome exploration by curious little hands. One fascinating exhibit showcases recovered artifacts from 400-year-old shipwrecks found in nearby waters.

The city also has more than a dozen art galleries and museums. Perhaps the best known collection of fine art is housed in the Art Museum of South Texas, as famous for the architecture of its stark white building as for what's inside. The Museum of Oriental Cultures features art of the Far East, and the Art Community Center showcases an eclectic collection of works by local artists.

Corpus Christi has some 10 major city parks with playgrounds and pools. Its open-air trolleys travel several interesting routes through the city, with a scenic bayfront tour on Saturdays. The Botanical Garden along the banks of Oso Creek has a nature trail and picnic area. It's free and you can find it southwest of the intersection of S. Staples at Yorktown.

Corpus Christi is one of the few seaports in the country whose business district extends to the marinas. You'll find some good restaurants in this area, including The Wayward Lady, a riverboat restaurant, on the L-Head; the Corpus Christi Dockside, a floating barge restaurant, on the People's Street T-Head; and the Lighthouse Bar & Grill on the Lawrence Street T-Head. Captain Boomer's, also on a floating barge, is said to have been a home for wayward boys run by evangelist Lester Roloff in days past. You get a good view of the city lights from there at night. Naturally, seafood is the specialty in most restaurants in town, but you can also find good Mexican food and that Texas favorite, barbecue.

If you tire of the salt water and sea air, head northwest 35 miles to **Lake Corpus Christi State Park,** where you'll find yourself at the largest freshwater lake in South Texas. You can fish, camp, boat, and swim there.

Note: See the section on Laredo for information on the **Tex-Mex Express** round-trip rail service from Corpus Christi to Laredo.

Padre Island National Seashore

9405 S. Padre Island Drive
Corpus Christi 78418
512-937-2621

It's a 15-minute drive across the Corpus Christi Bay to Padre Island. It is said the "Isla Blanca" (white island) was discovered by the Spanish conquistador Alvarez Alonzo de Piñeda as he plied the waters of the Gulf. Legend has it that he sailed into Corpus Christi Bay on the festival day of that name, in 1519. After that, Spanish, Portuguese, English, and French buccaneers, including Hernan Cortez and Jean Lafitte, dropped anchor in the bay. Today, treasure hunters equipped with metal detectors look for the buried treasure rumored to be buried on Padre and Mustang Islands, but they are more likely to come up with sand dollars than Spanish doubloons.

Padre Island's 110 miles of beaches include an 80-mile stretch of natural shoreline and the Padre Island National Seashore has a visitor's pavilion and camping facilities. Malaquite Beach, within the national seashore, has an observation tower where you get a bird's eye view of the island and bay. Public beaches are also found on the island, with excellent facilities.

Fredericksburg

The Fredericksburg you visit today feels more like a theme village from an amusement park than it does an actual city. Here you will find old-world German bakeries and biergartens, old-world German dress shops and museums, and a plethora of bed and breakfast homes around town. Stroll the length of Main St., and you'll get a true feel for the tradition of Fredericksburg's German heritage.

The restored **Old Dietz Bakery,** built in 1876 (312 E. Main) is interesting, but don't miss the actual **Dietz Bakery** (218 E. Main) down the block—known for a variety of fresh pastries, bread, and cookies. The doors stay open as long as there is anything left to sell Tuesday through Saturday. Drop by the delightful **Old Fredericksburg Bank** (120 E. Main) and the **Vereins Kirche Archives** (100 block of W. Main) where you will get a feel for the town's history, and directly behind the Vereins Kirche, take time to see the **Pioneer Place Garden,** a tiny green haven that sports a beautiful old wooden waterwheel. Troop down to **Oma Koock's** (312 W. Main), an excellent German restaurant that now occupies the original limestone building that began life as a hardware store.

In the 300 block of W. San Antonio, you'll find two churches that demand attention: the new **St. Mary's**

Church of 1906 and the **Marien Kirche,** the old St. Mary's, dating back to 1860. In all their Gothic splendor, the stone spire and delicate exterior work are transplants straight from the old country. **Scwettmann's Taxidermy** (305 W. Main) held a great attraction for our group. The collection behind glass includes buffalo, jackalope, deer, turkey and ostrich among others.

It is said that in this town people aren't Democratic or Republican, but they are patrons of either the Fredericksburg Bakery (141 E. Main) or the Dietz. With either, plan to arrive before noon or you'll have nothing but empty display cases staring at you.

Fredericksburg has grown famous for its homemade fudge—all five varieties—and other chocolate candies. So it couldn't hurt to wander by Fredericksburg Fudge (138 E. Main, 915-997-8913).

If you are planning an overnight stay in one of the many inns here, contact Bed and Breakfast of Fredericksburg (102 S. Cherry, 915-997-4712). Because B&B of Fredericksburg provides information on a variety of local accommodations, both old and new, you can save a lot of time when asking prices and policies on children. Other such services include Gastehaus Schmidt (501 Main, 915-997-5612).

For a real thrill, take the kids to this hands-on museum at the Admiral Nimitz State Historical Site in Fredericksburg with its many WWII relics.

Admiral Nimitz Center

328 E. Main
512-997-4379
Hours: 8 a.m.–5 p.m., daily.
Fredericksburg 78624
Admission charged.

Named for native son Chester W. Nimitz, who rose to the rank of admiral in the U.S. Navy during World War II and led a victorious Pacific campaign, this museum is housed in the restored boat-shaped hotel that was built by Chester's grandfather. Exhibits include photos, mementos of the Nimitz career, and plenty of history on WWII in the Pacific. Adjacent to the museum is the Japanese Peace Garden, which was a gift from Japan during the U.S. Bicentennial and built by Japanese artists sent here from Japan.

Enchanted Rock State Park

Rt 4 Box 170
Fredericksburg 78624
915-247-3903
Hours: Gates open at 7 a.m. and close at 10 p.m., daily.
Admission charged.
How to get there: Take FM 965 north from Fredericksburg 20 miles to the park entrance. Watch for signs.

From the shady park at the base of Enchanted Rock, the feat of climbing to the top may look too much for a Sunday hike. Don't let it scare you off: this may be the friendliest boulder in the state. It's definitely the largest. There is a marked summit hike that is reasonable when taken slowly. Kids will want to try to race to the top, but half the pleasure of the climb is remembering to stop and turn around and get a good look at the surrounding Hill Country. The climb takes about 45 minutes to an hour, and along the way you'll surely pass and be passed by all ages of hikers. There are plenty of good stopping places with a bit of shade and always a breeze. Lesser formations in the 100-square miles of Enchanted Rock State Park are diagrammed in the park map you'll get at the entrance. On a clear summer night when the moon is out, there is easily enough light to hike to the summit of Enchanted Rock and spend some time star-gazing. Enchanted rock is the second largest batholith in the United States, behind Georgia's Stone Mountain.

The park at the base sports an active, clear creek that is deep enough for cooling off but not for true swimming. Designated as a state natural area, Enchanted Rock offers only the basics to campers: primitive campsites, grills, running water and restrooms.

Pioneer Memorial Museum

309 W. Main
Fredericksburg 78624
512-997-2835
Hours: 10 a.m.–5 p.m., Mon.–Sat, 1 p.m.– 5 p.m., Sun., May–Labor Day; 10 a.m.–5 p.m., Sat., 1 p.m.–5 p.m., Sun., Labor Day–April. Admission charged.

With a heavy German influence, the tools, furniture, and clothing on display offer an intimate look at the hardships and triumphs pioneers to the area faced. The museum is comprised of five buildings: two period homes, one barn, one Sunday house and our favorite, the Fire Department Museum that features a replica of the original fire station, a turn-of-the-century hand pumper, a hose cart—and all are still in working order.

Johnson City

The area around Johnson City is rife with reminders of our thirty-sixth president. In fact you may get confused with all the Lyndon Baines Johnson parks and historical sites that abound. The LBJ National Historical Park is here in Johnson City. The LBJ National Historical Site and the LBJ State Historical Park are west of Johnson City in Stonewall.

LBJ National Historical Park

512-868-7128
Hours: 9 a.m.–5 p.m. daily except Christmas and New Year's Day. Admission free.
How to get there: The visitors center is on G Street one block south of U.S. Hwy 290 between 8th and 9th streets.

What is today Johnson City did not exist when LBJ's boyhood home came into the hands of his great-uncle Tom Johnson. The one-story white frame house protected by a frail picket fence was Johnson's home from 1914 to 1934. With his political career blossoming, Johnson hosted his first political rally here. The house has since been fully restored and furnished with Johnson family heirlooms and other pieces from the period. The house gives a warm, lived-in feeling with books and toys lying around the room Lyndon shared with brother Sam. Tours are available and the attending rangers are very knowledgeable on the subject of our late president. One block to the west is the Old Ranch, once the home of LBJ's grandfather. There is plenty of Johnson family history plus an actual chuckwagon and blacksmithing shop. An excellent excursion for kids.

Pedernales Falls State Park

Rt 1 Box 31A
Johnson City 78636
512-868-7304
Admission charged.
How to get there: Take U.S. Hwy 290 West to FM 2766. Turn east and follow the signs. Located 10 miles east of Johnson City.

The banks of the Pedernales River inside the park happen to include an unexpected stretch of clean, fine sand, ideal for sunning after wading and tubing. The clear waters of the river spread out over the rocks and spill across a couple of natural dams. The park landscape is packed with scrub, cedar and oak trees. There are plenty of campsites, shower-equipped restrooms, great fishing spots, and shaded picnic areas, but the big attraction is the river. Get ready for a beautiful sunset (or sunrise if you're camping overnight): a fine mist hangs over the water and the valley holds onto the moisture well into the morning hours. The half-mile nature trail troops you through one of the park's most scenic overlooks (another sunset favorite). Don't miss Twin Falls, runoff of two creeks as they meet before entering the Pedernales. Reservations for campsites are suggested, especially March through November.

Kerrville

Kerrville's claim to fame, outside her beautiful perch among the foothills, are the Spring and Fall music festivals held 16 miles south of town, off Texas Hwy 16, in Quiet Valley Ranch. Held in May and September over Memorial and Labor Day weekends, the festivals will entertain both adults and children (512-257-3600). Admission is definitely charged. For a quieter excursion, consider Kerrville's annual Texas State Arts and Crafts Fair held the last two weekends in May at Schreiner College (head east on Texas Hwy 27 three miles). Admission is charged.

Cowboy Artists of America Museum

1550 Bandera Hwy
Kerrville 78028
512-896-2553
Hours: Open daily June–August; Tues.–Sun., Sept.–May.
Admission charged.
How to get there: From Main St. (Texas Hwy 27) turn left onto Texas
*   Hwy 16, go across the Guadalupe River. Head south on Texas Hwy*
*   173 at the edge of town, watch for signs for the Museum.*

My pre-teen bunch absolutely insisted that we stop here first. The museum is the only one that exhibits the paintings and sculpture of living artists recognized for their work in Western American Realism. Take time to look around the building. The museum is done in historic Boveda brick domes, with a full explanation of the process presented inside, and the front garden entry is in limestone laced with imposing timbers. From the Museum store we brought home prints of several of the works on display and managed to knock a few names off our respective Christmas lists.

Kerrville State Park

2385 Bandera Hwy
Texas Hwy 173
Kerrville 78028
512-257-5392
Hours: Open at all times.
Admission charged.

Fronting the icy waters of the Guadalupe River, Kerrville State Park encompasses 500 acres of beautifully wooded Hill Country. Swimming, wading, tubing, and fishing are all options from the park. A network of hiking trails links shady picnic grounds. Sheltered and screened campsites are also available.

Kingsville

King Ranch

Kingsville 78363
512-592-6411
Hours: 8:30 a.m.–5 p.m., daily.
Admission free.
How to get there: Take Hwy 141 off either Hwy 77 or Hwy 281, west
*   of Kingsville to the Santa Gertrudis Division.*

Just about everybody has heard of the King Ranch and know it is the biggest in the country. How big? Well, most of the land south of Kingsville to Corpus Christi is part of it, comprising an area the size of the state of Rhode Island. Apart from its size, the Ranch is also famous for developing the first native American breed of cattle, the Santa Gertrudis. What may not be so commonly known is that it also developed the cattle prod, cattle dipping vats, its own breed of quarterhorses and two types of range grasses. Besides grazing some 60,000 head of cattle, the ranch plants 37,400 acres of cotton, and has 2,730 oil and gas wells.

The Ranch is divided into four geographically separate divisions: the Santa Gertrudis division, west of Kingsville; Laureles, east of Kingsville; Encino, south of Falfurrias, and Norias, south of Kingsville and located on both sides of

Hwy 77. At the Norias division the old-time roundup with cowboys on horseback remains a tradition. (Modern methods of rounding up cattle, using trucks, pens, and even helicopters, can't be used there because of the dense brush.)

The Santa Gertrudis Division contains the ranch headquarters and is the only section open to the casual visitor. At the entrance a self-guided cassette can be rented, and it takes about an hour to drive through the 12-mile loop. You'll pass through ebony trees and date palms and cross the Santa Gertrudis Creek, the most reliable source of water for many miles around. The road goes by pastures, pens, windmills, the auction pen area, stables and also past the old family residence, the Big House.

The ranch had a modest beginning with Richard King's purchase in 1853 of 15,500 acres of "worthless" land for $300. By the time of King's death, his holdings amounted to 1.2 million acres.

The ranch is a successful blending of the cultures of Mexico and Texas, still so much a part of South Texas. The business end of it is strictly American, with its reliance on computers and modern methods of ranch management, while the Hispanic values come through in the emphasis on loyalty, family, and dedication to the land. English is the language of the office; Spanish, the language of the range.

King's youngest daughter Alice married the ranch's manager and legal counsel, Robert Kleberg. Today his great-grandson, Stephen "Tio" Kleberg, runs the ranch. Far from sitting in a remote office, the Klebergs are out there on horseback alongside the ranch hands, indistinguishable from them in old hats and roughened jeans.

The Klebergs have through much of the history of the ranch been land rich and cash poor, and they still live in relative austerity. The huge family residence, known as the Big House, stands empty and is used only for meetings. To their credit, all the land was acquired legally—not a robber baron among them.

King Ranch is one of the last strongholds of what the Texas myth is all about, and shouldn't be missed.

Laredo

Laredo Convention and Visitor's Council
2310 San Bernardo
P.O. Box 790
Laredo 78040
512-722-9895

Now a burgeoning metropolis of over 100,000 inhabitants, Laredo's old section remains preserved around the old plaza in the heart of town. The **Villa de San Agustin Historical Zone** includes about 15 blocks of the old city. Start out at the plaza and begin your explorations with the San Agustin Church. Nearby, the elegant La Posada Hotel was formerly the 1916 Laredo High School building. Next to the hotel is the adobe capitol building of the ill-fated Republic of the Rio Grande, which was in precarious existence for about 283 days. After Texas won independence from Mexico in 1836, Laredo remained part of no-man's-land. A group of Mexicans unhappy with Santa Anna's government declared in 1840 that the area bordering the Rio Grande was an independent republic and named Laredo as its capital. Its flag waved until Santa Anna's forces overran the town. Now, the old capitol building is a museum with furnishings of the time, Indian artifacts, and memorabilia from old Laredo families.

On the southwest corner of the plaza is the old **Bruni Home,** built in the 1880s, now a bar and restaurant. These are just a few of the old buildings to be seen in the historical district.

For shopping or just looking, browse in the new market off the main square.

The **Fort McIntosh/Nuevo Santander Museum** is located at the present site of Laredo Junior College and Laredo State University. There you can explore the old fort's guardhouse, chapel, warehouse and commissary, now a museum. The fort was in use from 1848 to 1946, first to guard against Indian attacks and later as a border patrol station.

Nuevo Laredo, Mexico

Across the border from Laredo.

Nuevo Laredo is another busy and populous border town. It and Laredo were the same community until the Mexican War, when 136 families started the new town of Nuevo Laredo.

For shopping, the **Mercado M. Herrera** features traditional Mexican market fare: baskets, weavings, souvenirs, pottery, leather goods, liquor, and jewelry. Nearby on the corner of Calles Guerrero and Victoria is Marti's, an elegant store with designer clothes, crystal, and other pricey items.

Children find the glass blowers lining Calle Guerrero endlessly fascinating. It is seventeen more blocks along

The most fascinating shopping on the border is offered by the Mexican markets with treasures for everyone of all ages.

Calle Guerrero to Vega's, which is a huge store that resembles a Mexican hacienda and specializes in fine furniture.

To see how the rich live, drive or hire a taxi to take you along Paseo Colon and enjoy the elegant mansions. Across from the plaza on the same street is the home of the Longorias, one of the wealthiest and most influential families in Nuevo Laredo. The church on the plaza was built by the Longorias, using statuary from Europe. Within the church is a museum filled with beautiful objects collected by the Longoria family on their European jaunts. The famous Cadillac Bar is on the corner of Calles Belden and Ocampo. It's been a popular eatery since 1926 and was renovated a couple of years ago.

If you'd like to spend the night across the border, try the popular El Rio Motor Hotel on the Reforma. It is very modern and the restaurant is excellent.

The Tex-Mex Express

512-722-6411 (Laredo)
512-289-1818 (Corpus Christi)
Hours: Train departs Laredo at 4 p.m. Fri., Sat., and Sun. It arrives in Corpus at 8:30 p.m. It leaves Corpus at 9:30 a.m. and arrives in Laredo at 1:30 p.m.
Admission: Round-trip and one-way tickets are reasonably priced. Call for reservations and fare information.

All aboard the renovated Tex-Mex Express for a ride to Corpus Christi! What better way to travel than by train, where you can get up and stretch your legs, sit back and watch the scenery, or take a snooze? The advantages are doubly obvious for those who travel with children. The four coaches and lounge car of the Tex-Mex Express were built in the early 1900s and renovated in 1986. Originally built for comfort, the vintage railcars now have the added advantages of air conditioning, piped in music, and, if you tire of the scenery, movies on videocassette. There's a lounge car equipped with a bar that serves sandwiches and snacks, too. The four-hour trip takes you through 157 miles of ranchland, oil fields, scrub brush, and an occasional field of wildflowers.

Prosperous citizens of Corpus Christi started this rail line in 1856, then Captains Richard King and Miflin Kenedy, later partners in the King Ranch empire, extended it. The route was completed to Laredo in 1881. In those days it made stops for every cowboy who flagged it down, or for passengers to pile out and engage in some hunting along the way. Nowadays, except for whistle stops in Hebbronville and Alice, it travels nonstop.

Luckenbach

This celebrated spot off FM 1376 courtesy of the late mayor, Hondo Crouch, is truly a diamond in the rough—and the locals work hard to keep it that way. By way of local attractions, there is one all-purpose general store with beer on tap out back and an enormous (for Luckenbach) dance floor. Kids may wonder why this spot is famous, but wandering around the vacancy is sort of fun. Notice the one

parking meter. It is even more interesting when one considers all the publicity showered on this garden spot by the likes of Waylon Jennings, Willie Nelson, and Jerry Jeff Walker. Stop long enough to grab a cold drink and peruse some of the announcements for upcoming events. Who could pass up a homegrown beer festival or a washer-toss championship?

New Braunfels

Landa Park

512-625-5818
Hours: Open year round.
No admission charges except for large groups reserving picnic grounds May–October.
How to get there: California Blvd heading south leads right into the park across the Comal River.

Stop here for a relaxing picnic or simply a stroll through. The headwaters of the Comal River make the setting even nicer; there is a miniature railroad, golf course, amusement park, a regulation-size playground, and paddleboats. A spring-fed swimming pool lined in natural stone is breathtaking—as much for the icy temperature of the water as for the beauty. Be careful getting in. If these waters are too much, Landa Park also sports a chlorine-and-cement version—just up the stairs. Kids tend to race back and forth be-

tween the two, making the day all the more adventure-packed.

Sophienburg Museum

401 W. Coll at Academy
512-629-1527
Hours: 10 a.m.–5 p.m., Mon.–Sat., 1–5 p.m., Sun.
Admission charged.

This hilltop perch was once the site of a fortress charged with the protection of New Braunfels. The museum here offers a commanding view of the surrounding territory. Inside the collection has matured from its early, more freeform days into a true cache of historical information. The extreme hardships suffered by settlers to the region and their surviving traditions are all chronicled in the New

Braunfels memorabilia. Even if only for the view, children love the visit.

Camp Warnecke

370 W. Lincoln
512-625-3710
New Braunfels 78130
Hours: 9 a.m.–10 p.m. daily, June through August; 9 a.m.–8 p.m., the rest of the year weather permitting.
Admission charged. Reservations recommended for cabins and motel rooms.
How to get there: Exit Lake McQueeny off IH 35, turn west on Seguin Ave. Ten blocks down, just past E. Garden St. is the entrance to the park. Follow the signs.

A perennial vacation tradition in Texas, Camp Warnecke exists to make full use of the nippy clear waters of the Comal River. It offers four-star tubing along the shortest river in the world (3.25 miles) plus swimming and sliding. The pace of the river is inconsistent, with smooth drifts in-terrupted by exciting rapids. The river never runs more than three and a half to four feet deep, but life jackets on the smaller kids are still a good idea and can be rented along with tubes at the front entrance. T-shirts, sun block, and dark glasses are all essential equipment for a day on the river.

The Guadalupe River

New Braunfels Chamber of Commerce
390 S. Seguin
New Braunfels 78130
512-625-2385
How to get there: Take Texas Hwy 46 west. Not too far outside the city, at the River Rd intersection, head north. You'll soon be in the heart of river-rat country.

Playing along the beautiful Guadalupe can be great fun: canoes, rafts, and inner tubes are all available for rental at reasonable rates (and usually include shuttle service to and

Photo courtesy of Tourism Division, Texas Department of Commerce

This group of happy rafters is wetting their feet in the cool waters of the Guadalupe River near New Braunfels.

from the river). For greenhorns to the area, there are expert outfitters ready to launch in-depth tours. For families with smaller children, this may be the smartest route.

Few other adventures can compare to navigating your own vessel—raft, tube, or canoe—down these waters. For long stretches, the river is calm and glassed-over. And then around the next bend you can hear the happy shouting and rush of the rapids tumbling brave souls out of their tubes. Kids tend to spend their time chasing and upending each other, while dyed-in-the-wool river rats know that peace lies in sitting back and allowing the Guadalupe to take you to your destination. Life jackets are a good idea for the littler ones, and there are even tubes that come attached to each other—perfect for close supervision of a child.

Port Isabel and South Padre Island

South Padre Island Tourist Bureau
600-A Padre Blvd
S. Padre Island 78597
512-943-6433

South Padre Island's surf and sand are fun for kids of all ages: build sand castles, fly kites on the beach, hunt for sea shells, play in the waves, rent a surfboard or windsurfer. You can also rent a three-wheeler and ride along the bay side of the island. For the less adventurous who want a quieter ride, there are bicycle surreys. A slow-moving tram makes a tour of the island every hour or so, free. You can get on or off at any place on the main island road. Jeremiah's Landing is a favorite with kids with its giant water slides and mini-golf.

If you like fishing, try your luck in the waters of Laguna Madre Bay from a boat, on foot, or from the fishing pier located on the old causeway. (Anchor the children with a rope if you're afraid they'll fall off the bridge.) On the island you can rent a boat and go deep-sea fishing.

A paddleboat, the *Isabella Queen*, is available for day or night tours of the bay. If you love sailing, small sailboats or Hobie-Cats are for rent. If you'd like to survey the entire area from the air, take a helicopter ride; or if you're over the age of 12, parasailing is available.

A public camping area and park with trailer hook-ups is available at the southern end of the island at the **Isla Blanca Park.** It's a public beach with lifeguards. Nearby is the **Pan American Marine Biology Lab,** which offers a free display of local plants and marine animals every afternoon except Saturday.

Near the causeway in Port Isabel, there's the *Lady Bea*, a shrimp boat up on blocks and open to the public as a museum. Children are usually fascinated by being aboard a real shrimp boat.

Also near the causeway is the old **Port Isabel lighthouse,** now open to the public and not too difficult a climb. The lighthouse was built in 1853 on the site of Fort Polk. Its lights guided incoming ships until 1905, when it was decommissioned. In 1952 the State of Texas opened it as a historical monument and the state's smallest state park.

The famous "Turtle Lady," otherwise known as Ila Loetscher, provides in her home at 5805 Gulf Boulevard a refuge for the endangered Kemp's Ridley sea turtle. This gracious octogenarian takes care of injured sea turtles there until they are ready to return to the sea. Twice a week Ila presents a free show and informal lecture on these gentle giants. Check with the South Padre Island Tourist Bureau for schedules or call 512-761-2544.

South Padre Island boasts an assortment of lodging and eating places for every taste and pocketbook, the former tending a bit toward the expensive side, since it is basically a tourist spot. Some favorite restaurants include the Jetty's at the southern tip of the island. It features an excellent view of beach, surf, and the ships entering and leaving the ship channel. It has a children's menu, and the prices are reasonable. Blackbeard's Restaurant is roomy and has good food, including many children's favorites. The Windjammers at the Hilton has an excellent breakfast buffet and offers special prices for children.

In Port Isabel, try the Fisherman's Inn on Hwy 100. Don't be turned off by its humble appearance. Definitely a family

Photo courtesy of South Padre Island Convention and Business Bureau

For a family vacation on the beach, South Padre Island has it all with every type of accommodation from budget to major chain hotels.

place, it also has good food and a down-home atmosphere. Its specialty is the bite-sized fried shrimp. If you finish the first serving (about 3 dozen) for $5.95, the second order costs only $1.

If you plan to stay overnight on the Island, make reservations in advance. The Bahia Mar Resort Hotel is on the beach and has a good restaurant. The Sea Island Hilton is possibly the best (and most expensive) place on the Island to stay for a family vacation, especially if you plan to stay a few days. If you get tired of the attractions of the beach, an activities director can guide you to an amazing variety of leisure pastimes: arts and crafts for children, swimming and wading pool games, and water exercise for the older crowd to name just a few. A clown works poolside teaching juggling, making balloon animals, and doing other clown-like things. Monday through Saturday evenings from 6 to 10, there's a kid's dinner and entertainment (children must be at least 5 to partake).

Rockport

Rockport-Fulton Tourist Association
P.O. Box 1482
Rockport 78382
512-729-2388

Rockport is said to have more resident artists than any other community its size in the country. Besides that, it is tiny, quaint and lovely. Downtown is still the center of activity, and its sidewalks are lined with artists' studios and galleries. A few blocks away is a neighborhood of old homes built before 1870.

Fulton Mansion

P.O. Box 1859
Fulton 78358
512-729-0386
Hours: 9 a.m.–11:30 a.m., 1 p.m.–4 p.m., Wed.–Sun.
Admission charged.
How to get there: Drive a few miles north of Rockport on Hwy 35 to the community of Fulton.

The George Ware Fulton Mansion is one of the top historic homes in the nation. Built in 1874 of French Second Empire design, the mansion has three stories and 19 rooms. The house is fascinating because Fulton had installed in it all the latest technological wonders of his time, including flush toilets and central heat.

The town of Lamar is north of Fulton on Hwy 35. Here you can gaze at **Texas' biggest live oak tree,** and probably the oldest, too. Estimated to be anywhere from 1,000 to 2,000 years old, the "Big Tree" has a circumference of 35 feet and is 44 feet high. It is reputed to have been the execution site of the cannibalistic Karankawa tribe and later used as a hanging tree.

Across the bay from Lamar is **Goose Island State Park,** with its facilities for camping, fishing, swimming, and picnicking.

San Antonio

San Antonio Convention and Visitors Center
P.O. Box 2277
San Antonio 78298
800-531-5700

Despite being the third largest city in Texas, San Antonio has held on to and nurtured an almost quaint notion of itself as the tiny Mexican mission it was in the early 1700s. This dream state exists in the middle of a stepped-up campaign on the part of local boosters and politicos to cast their city in the role of a sophisticated, urban mecca. No matter which image you subscribe to, the Bexar county seat is great for a weekend of exploring.

Our advice is to keep a map on your person at all times; it won't take long to get a feel for the layout of the city, and try not to get discouraged when the street you're on changes names unexpectedly.

The Alamo

Alamo Plaza at Alamo St.
512-225-1391
Hours: 9 a.m.–5:30 p.m., Mon.–Sat., 10 a.m.–5:30 p.m., Sun. Closed Christmas Day.
Admission free.
How to get there: Take IH 37 to the HemisFair exit, turn west on Commerce St. and north on Alamo.

"Why is it sitting in the middle of downtown? There's supposed to be a big open field and lots of tumbleweeds." Our group was unprepared for the mission of today, standing diminutively against the backdrop of the city grown up around it. But it only takes walking through the front doors and into the cool, history-drenched interior to get a sense of the battle once fought here. Only the chapel of the Alamo remains today, but it is a powerful and fascinating experience to stand on the uneven stone floor and conjure up scenes of the famous final battle. The many exhibits include actual weapons, clothing, and letters and documents from the likes of Davy Crockett and William Travis.

Established in 1718, the Alamo was the first of the missions constructed by the Spaniards to educate and convert the Indians. The famous legend of the Alamo grew around a thirteen-day stand for independence made by less than 200 Texans against the Mexican army.

The Daughters of the Republic of Texas are charged with the care and upkeep of the Alamo. Daily tours of the mission and the lush, shady grounds are informative and well done, although with all there is to occupy the imagination of kids, you may want to just let them explore on their own. With older kids, just synchronize everyone's watches, agree on a time to rendezvous and meet out in front by the landmark flagpole. We've been back a half-dozen times now, and each visit holds new discoveries. (See *The Alamo and Other Texas Missions to Remember,* Lone Star Books, Houston, 1984.)

The Missions

Following the establishment of the Alamo in 1718, four other missions were built in what is today the city of San Antonio. All are still standing, most in their original form, and offer a distinct perspective on a yet incomplete history of the early missions. Established to further the territory of Spain, the missions offered converted Indians virtual safety from raids of hostile rivals. We visited all five (including the Alamo) in a day, and though each site is worth seeing, Mission San Jose was the clear favorite after the Alamo. The Mission Trail is clearly marked beginning downtown at South St. Mary Street. You'll need to turn right when you get in the vicinity of Roosevelt Park (take Playmoor or Biering Street) and then turn left onto Roosevelt. Self-guided tour brochures are available at each mission.

Mission Concepcion
807 Mission Rd at Mitchell
512-532-3158
Hours: 9 a.m.–6 p.m., daily.
Admission free.

As the oldest unrestored stone church building in the country, Mission Concepcion is also one of the most beautiful. Founded originally in 1716, nearly 40 years passed before the mission was opened for good. The structure has been left virtually untouched; take note of the interior adornments—they are all the "real McCoy."

Mission San Jose
6539 San Jose at Roosevelt
512-922-2731
Hours: 9 a.m.–6 p.m., daily.
Admission free.

The Queen of the Missions, San Jose offers the most complete sense of what life was like for the Indians and missionaries. The complex, which is in various stages of restoration, includes Indian dwellings, Spanish settlements, the monastery and church, and a large granary. This setting invites young imaginations to run wild. Take a look at the ornate adobe grist mill just outside the north wall, dating back to the late 1700s.

Sundays bring interdenominational masses conducted in the chapel. Complete with mariachis, the services are serene and peaceful and the strolling musicians stick around after mass for some impromptu serenading.

Mission San Juan Capistrano
9101 Graf St.
512-532-5840
Hours: 9 a.m.–6 p.m., daily.
Admission free.

Used today as a parish church (evening mass offered daily), San Juan is a peaceful haven nearly covered over with trees and shrubbery.

Mission San Francisco de la Espada
1004 Espada Rd
512-627-2021
Hours: 9 a.m.–6 p.m., daily.
Admission free.

Here is the most picturesque and charming of the whole mission trail. Known simply as Mission Espada (Mission of the Sword), you will be surprised at how different this structure feels from the others along the trail. The grounds are almost completely grass-covered, with only an occasional live oak or huisache standing sentry. Unfortunately, picnicking is not allowed.

HemisFair Plaza

Bounded by Alamo, IH 37, Durango and Market
512-299-8570
Admission free.

Site of the 1968 World's Fair held in San Antonio, HemisFair Plaza houses the Tower of the Americas, Institute of Texan Cultures, Instituto Cultural Mexicano, and the Convention Center in addition to a good assortment of restaurants, museums, art galleries, a theater, and more. During the construction of the fair grounds, plenty of historic old homes and buildings were renovated making for an exceptional stroll down the bricked-over, tree-lined walkways.

Tower of the Americas
E. Market St. and Bowie
512-223-3101
Hours: 10 a.m.–11 p.m., daily.
Admission charged.

From up here you can see the effects of the Austin-San Antonio corridor campaign: San Antonio is enormous. Great views of the gateway to the Hill Country and downtown's interesting mix of old buildings tucked in between new megastructures are yours from the tower. For the sheer experience, we decided to try the restaurant. Lunch was not stellar, but the view certainly was.

Institute of Texan Cultures
Durango and Bowie
512-226-7651
Hours: 9 a.m.–5 p.m., Tue.–Sun.
Admission free.

A trip through the Institute can nearly eclipse the Alamo and, because of its scope and diversity, this stop should not be missed by those of you with children.

No run-of-the-mill museum, the Institute is a continuous multi-media event. The history of Texas and the people that have been along for the ride are covered in the Institute's excellent rotation of exhibits. Just about any ethnic extraction you may claim is represented in the films, demonstrations, displays and slides.

Being keenly aware of its audience, the Institute's curators have gone overboard to capture and hold the kids' attention. Exhibits move and talk and ask questions—and answer yours. The stark contrast between beautiful armor worn by a Spanish conquistador and the scientific wonder of the Apollo 8 command module mark the Institute's range. The life of early settlers, the challenge faced by immigrants, the melding of divergent cultures are represented.

Don't leave without seeing the spectacular Dome Show, an electronic, multiple-screen, mixed media presentation that is part light show and part hologram and is one of the most popular attractions with kids. Other sights that set the Institute apart include the state's earliest transportation contraptions, extensive Indian exhibits, enormous and primitive weaving looms, ethnic clothing from the middle of last century, and early books and newspapers.

The annual Texas Folklife Festival, hosted by the Institute, is one of the state's finest fairs. Held in early August, the four-day festival runs amok with obscure, ethnic activities, food booths, craft demonstrations, and long-forgotten dances. A marvelous mixture of music, food, dancing, art and people is yours for a small admission.

Brackenridge Park

Entrance at Broadway and Tuleta, and at Mulberry at N. St. Mary's
512-229-3000
Hours: Open at all times.
Admission free.
How to get there: From the McAllister Frwy, take the Brackenridge
Park exit and follow the signs. An alternative route: take Broadway
to the Witte Museum and turn west; follow the signs.

This is picnic territory, so come prepared with sunglasses, visors, or sunblock.

As one of the city's most attractive spots, Brackenridge tends to stay full of people on weekends and holidays. It is no coincidence that kids love this place; activities here include riding stables, the San Antonio Zoo, Sunken Gardens, a golf course, a playground, and a miniature train (the Brackenridge Eagle takes you on a twenty-minute circuit around the park). It is tough to squeeze everything the park has to offer into one day, but it's been done. To begin, get your bearings by hopping the sky ride over the park. After you've got the lay of the land, better get busy.

San Antonio Zoological Gardens and Aquarium
3903 N. St. Mary's
512-734-7183
Hours: 9:30 a.m.–5 p.m., daily, Nov.–Mar., 9:30 a.m.–6:30 p.m.,
daily, Apr.–Oct.
Admission charged.

Especially for kids, this is one of San Antonio's best attractions. After a few years of an informal existence more as a collection of rare animals, the San Antonio Zoo was established in 1929. Holding its own as one of the top ten zoos in the country, the SAZ was built on the site of an old rock quarry and makes excellent use of the remaining ledges and bluffs. The zoo feels authoritative with its authentic rolling terrain and extensive landscaping so well suited to the animals. If so inclined, as kids usually are, drop by the reptile house early in your visit as it closes at 1 p.m.

Be sure to see the Animal Nursery. A highly successful addition to the zoo, the nursery is overrun with cuddly, newborn creatures, some of which are old enough to pet.

There are those who can get through the zoo quickly, but the wiser choice would be to spend at least the morning with the animals and then break for a picnic in the park. After lunch you may hear some pleading to go horseback riding, because by this time there have been plenty of signs for the stables and people have probably casually sauntered by on horses. One good compromise might be elephant rides available on weekends. For 75 cents per person, the rides take just a fraction of the time.

Sunken Gardens
3800 N. St. Mary's
512-299-3000
Hours: Dawn to dusk, daily.
Admission free.

Winding through a colorful overgrowth of lush, almost tropical flowers are narrow walkways, surprisingly deep ponds and precarious rock bridges. Originally, this was a limestone rock quarry, thus the many levels and ledges.

River Walk (Paseo del Rio)

Downtown
Hours: Open at all times.
Admission free.

Here you'll find the heart of the city. The San Antonio River, running right through the center of town, provides one and a half miles of romance and elegance, fun discoveries, and a few of the city's most beautiful stretches. Lining the river are tall oak and cypress, a host of sidewalk cafes, art galleries, ice cream parlors, specialty shops, and a bookstore or two. Situated ten or fifteen feet below street level, the River Walk takes you under century-old bridges and up and down oddly placed stairs.

On any given afternoon along the river, the atmosphere is a lazy one. Outdoor cafes are the perfect spot to do some serious people-watching as crowds stroll past. As the sun sets, the pace begins to quicken and all manner and decibel of music drifts out from the hefty assortment of restaurants and clubs.

The River Walk is San Antonio's crowning attraction. Any number of walking tours have been devised for exploring each nuance of the river, but just go with your instincts. As with any group larger than two, be sure to keep an eye on each other to avoid getting separated.

San Antonio's beautiful and exciting River Walk meanders for several miles through the heart of this old and historic city.

Kids get a kick out of dodging in and out of the oncoming crowds, but a warning here on just how narrow the walkway can get at certain points: we had to fish a frightened, embarrassed six-year-old out of the water (and I'm sure he would have pulled his older brother in with him if he could have).

For most every holiday during the year, there is a special celebration along the River Walk. The most spectacular takes place during the Christmas season when the river is lined with luminarias and the trees are draped in tiny colored lights. The effect is surrealistic, romantic, and just plain exciting.

Throughout the year, paddleboats can be rented for tooling around on the river. Available by the hour, this is a fun way to see all the activity and not get stuck in the inevitable traffic jams along the walk. And in case you're in need of some R&R, group excursion boats run all the time and all you're required to do is climb on and enjoy.

When you're ready for a change of scenery, head for **Market Street** (overpasses carry street names) where in the 200 block, four blocks west of the river, you'll find the Main Library Building, which is now home to the **Hertzberg Circus**

Collection. The miniature displays provide a delightful history of the Barnum & Bailey legend. Most intriguing is the collection of circus costumes, old photographs and random circus trivia and treasure.

Market Square itself is bounded by Santa Rosa, Dolorosa, and W. Commerce just east of IH 35.

The central mall of Market Square comes alive on weekends with live music—some mariachi, some contemporary—and small but excellent food stands. For one-man operations, you can't find better fajitas, tamales, barbacoa, menudo, or chorizo.

In the shops, galleries, and eateries surrounding the square, there is a definite Mexican flair. Try the specialty fruit drinks prepared at cafes in the district made from fresh papaya, pineapple, mango, tangerine, lemon and lime.

Have you been to **Mi Tierra?** Kids absolutely eat this place up. In the heart of Market Square, it sits at 218 Produce row. Because no reservations are taken, you're left up to the hands of fate on getting in the door. Time your arrival for off-peak hours (which at this 24-hour circus, are few). From strolling mariachis who could pass for clowns to the wild Mexican decor and overstuffed bakery case at the front of the restaurant, this is a haven for the young. The Mexican food is good, enhanced greatly by the atmosphere and constant commotion.

La Villita

Bounded by the river, Nueva, S. Alamo and S. Presa
512-299-8610
Hours: Open at all times.
Admission free.

From early June to late August at the Arneson Theater, the Fiesta Noche del Rio lights up the open-air amphitheater with colorful shows featuring native Mexican and Spanish music, singers and dancers. Shows are scheduled for several days through the week. One mariachi band invited the children gathered around to come dance to their music. Once the shyness wore off, the kids joined in and had a great time.

Brooks Aerospace Medical School

512-536-3234
Free admission. Call for tour information, tours scheduled three days a week according to requests. No unscheduled visitors accepted. Children must be at least 10 years old to go on the tour.
How to get there: Take IH 37 south to Military Drive, turn east. The School of Aerospace Medicine will be on the south side of the highway.

This is a hard-core, educational tour dressed up in sheer adventure. Brooks offers an up-close look at the maze of facilities used to test and train astronauts. The two-and-a-half-hour tour takes you through the centrifuge, the zero-gravity chambers, the hyperbaric chambers, and the flight simulators. Called a Medical School, Brooks was set up to measure the effects of space on the human condition. You'll thoroughly enjoy the experience and so will the kids. Also on the grounds is the Ed White Museum, which includes the oldest World War I hangar in existence, and is now a National Historical Landmark. NASA exhibits are on display along with a detailed account of the space program. One of the original planes flown in and out of Brooks, the Jenny, is on display alongside photos of Brooks cadet Charles Lindbergh. Count on a pooped bunch at the end of the tour.

Buckhorn Hall of Horns

Lone Star Brewery, 600 Lone Star at Mission Rd
512-226-8301
Hours: 9:30 a.m.–5 p.m., daily.
Admission charged.
How to get there: From IH 37 South, head west on Texas Hwy 90. Exit Mission Rd and go south.

Originally, the Buckhorn was a saloon that approached Ripley's status with the largest collection of antlers and horns in the world. The highlight of the 106-year-old collection is the intricate antler chandelier that hangs in the center of the main hall. The collection is joined by the hall of feathers, the hall of fins, and a wild walk through display cases filled with nature's oddities. The youngest member of our entourage complained that he thought we'd get to see the kind of horns that blow and make noise—but he was eventually happy to be eye to eye with a stuffed two-headed calf. Inside the tasting hall soft drinks are available. Bring a camera—there are many good spots for photos on the grounds.

Stonewall

LBJ State Historical Park

Two miles east of town, follow the signs along Park Rd 1
512-644-2252
Hours: 9 a.m.–5 p.m., daily. Hours may vary during summer months.
Admission free.

The only way to get all the way around this collection of President Johnson's life is to hop on one of the tours. Sign up for a free tour at the visitor center at the entrance to the site. The park covers about 700 acres, including the reconstructed Johnson birthplace, the one-room school house LBJ attended, the Johnson family cemetery, the ranch house that Senator and Mrs. Lady Bird bought in 1951 and an interesting drive in and around the LBJ ranch. By the time your tour is complete, there is no doubt but that you'll know a lot about the Johnson clan.

Just to the east of the visitor center is the **Sauer-Beckman Farm,** an operating historical farm with equipment, animals, buildings, and crops common to area farms in the early 1900s. This is easily one of the park's finest exhibits. Employees dressed for the part, are on hand to show visitors how they perform the daily work of running the farm. The changing seasons bring new chores: the garden is planted in the spring, fall is taken up with butchering. Christmastime on the farm includes an old-fashioned holiday tree with treats for all visitors.

Fronting the cool, rippling creek that runs through the park, there is a mile-and-a-half-long nature trail. Well-shaded and cool, the trail wraps around wildlife enclosures that house white-tail deer, bison, longhorn cattle, javelinas and wild turkeys. A playground awaits children near the parking area, and other recreational options include a wading pool for kids, an olympic-size swimming pool, tennis courts, picnic areas and a baseball diamond. Camping is not allowed. If you haven't gotten your fill of the Johnson saga, head east on U.S. Hwy 290 to Johnson City to see the **LBJ National Historical Park**.

Vanderpool

Lost Maples State Natural Area

Station C Rt
Vanderpool 78885
512-966-3413
Hours: 8 a.m.–10 p.m. daily, for day use, overnight camping allowed.
Admission charged.
How to get there: Take FM 187 north four miles from Vanderpool.

Known for the renegade pack of the rare Uvalde bigtooth maple trees that line one stretch of the park, Lost Maples offers excellent camping, hiking, exploration, and bird-watching. During the first half of November each year you can count on these maples to flame red, yellow, gold, and orange. The park is geared toward nature study and careful exploring of the area. Eleven miles of nature trails wind along the Sabinal Canyon. Campsites—both improved and primitive—are available, and reservations need to be made way in advance for those November weekends.

Wimberley

The town square is lined with antique shops, cafes and galleries of various types. It's fun just to get out and walk the perimeter.

Pioneer Town

512-947-2517
Hours: 10 a.m.–10 p.m., June–Aug.; hours vary Sept.–May.
Admission is free. Parking is 25 cents.
How to get there: Take River Rd west one mile and follow the signs.

Down to the finest detail, this re-creation of a 19th-century Texas town is entertaining, if fictitious. Your parking fee includes the price of the quick tour around town; you'll see the hotel, ice-cream parlor, the saloon, the blacksmith shop, opera house, bank, barber shop, printing office, gun shop, of course a jail, and even an old cafe dishing up pioneer portions. For those unable to weather pioneer living, there is also a well-stocked cemetery.

Kids are invited to ride the little train around town and recently, an arcade filled with games was added. On an ever-changing schedule, there is entertainment in the evening at the opera house. Acts ranging from old-fashioned medicine shows to barbershop quartets to gay nineties reviews begin at 8:15. For those staying around for the show, plenty of good food can be found in Wimberley. With kids, we've found excellent service at the Cypress Creek Cafe (Town Square, 512-847-2515).

A scenic Hill Country drive not to miss is along a stretch known as Devil's Backbone. Take FM 12 south from town to FM 32, turn right and give yourself eight miles of understated Texas beauty. Round trip is about 24 miles.

One of the points of pride in the area is a swimming spot on Cypress Creek known as the **Blue Hole**. From the town square, head out of town on Kyle Road past several offices, a lumber yard and finally, the cemetery. Just past the cemetery, turn left and follow the signs. Admission is charged.

Rope swings hang from trees, inner tubes float beneath the overhanging cypress. This is a Hill Country haven. The waters are cool when you first jump in, but you'll adjust in no time. For the sunbathers among you there are a few choice sunning spots, but remember, the Blue Hole is best for swimming.

WEST &
NORTHWEST

- Dalhart

Amarillo
- Canyon

Lubbock •

• Carlsbad

Abilene

Midland
• Odessa

• El Paso

Pecos
Monahans

• San Angelo

Balmorhea •

• Fort Stockton

Fort Davis •

Marfa • • Alpine

• Presidio

Big Bend

Abilene

Everyone has heard of Abilene on the old cattle trail. Like other old cattle towns, Abilene was once a rough and tumble place, but it is now a pleasant, modern city thanks to oil, gas, agriculture, and the military. There are many things to amuse the children for a few hours or a few days in this city and environs.

The **Observatory at Hardin-Simmons University,** the **Heritage Museum** at Dyess Air Force Base (915-797-4266), and **Oscar Rose Park** (7th and Mockingbird) with playgrounds, picnicking, pool, fine arts museum, etc. are worth visits, especially on a rainy day.

Nelson Park and the Zoological Gardens

Near junction of Loop 322 and TX 36
915-676-6222
Hours: Dawn to dusk, daily, year round.
Admission charged.

This is a true animal lovers' zoo—it doesn't have the commercialism of most zoos, and so it possesses a special charm, a sense of being a visitor in the animals' home.

The zoo is carefully laid out according to the natural habitats of the animals, and so you can visit the African Veld, the Australian Outback, South American rain forests, and so on, and find the animals living next door to their natural neighbors. There is also an excellent collection of exotic birds.

One of the most delightful single exhibits is the giraffes. A bridge over the moat where the tall animals are enclosed brings a child "eyeball to eyeball" with these towering creatures, an experience children don't often have. And of course they will also enjoy a variety of cats, grazing herd animals, reptiles and, in season, animal babies.

Nearby is **Zoo World,** a family entertainment complex whose claim to fame is a swimming pool with a sandy beach—a rare sight in West Texas. So when the kids are tired of looking at the animals, a picnic lunch and a swim are just the thing to revive their spirits.

Buffalo Gap Historic Village

14 miles south on US Hwy 89
915-572-3365 or 915-572-3572
Hours: Tues–Sun., Apr.–Oct.; weekends only the rest of year.
Admission charged.

Buffalo Gap Historic Village is one of the hidden treasures of this region; it has been carefully and tastefully developed for visitors. One of the first things you will notice will be the streets lined with live oak trees, a rare and beautiful sight in this treeless country.

The village contains all the amenities of village life, plus a few modern-day comforts, such as Mulberry Market, with interesting, off-beat shopping. There is a historic village, where the restored original buildings include the first Taylor county courthouse and jail, the Museum of the Old

For an authentic old "shoot 'em up" western town, the place to go is Buffalo Gap Historic Village.

West, an antique shop, and a variety of interesting restaurants (a good modern addition) with all kinds of food.

There are always several special things going on, such as craftspersons demonstrating their techniques, which are sure to fascinate the children. The workers and guides are generally in pioneer dress, adding to the flavor of having stepped back in time; they are also unfailingly polite and cheerful and willing to answer questions.

On your way back to town, stop by **Abilene State Recreation Area,** the site of an old Comanche Indian campground, to picnic, watch the birds, take a nature walk, or swim.

Fort Griffin State Historical Park

US Hwy 283
15 miles north of Albany

Here are the ruins of an old fort built to provide a little protection for the explorers, soldiers, prospectors, trappers, English would-be investors, and, finally, pioneer farm and ranch families who passed through here on their way to start new lives. They needed protection, for every gunfighter, outlaw, and renegade in the Old West visited Fort Griffin at one time or another. It was a wild, rough-and-tumble town, scene of poker games at which thousands of dollars changed hands, drunken brawls, and gunfights. The Visitors' Center will provide information, maps, and answers to questions.

Try to plan your trip to see the **Fort Griffin Fandangle,** a locally-produced historical drama in which some of the players are the third generation of their families to appear in it. The Fandangle is held the last two weekends of June, Thursday through Saturday. (Reservations are a must.) (See *Frontier Forts of Texas*, Lone Star Books, Houston, 1986.)

Amarillo

Amarillo Convention and Visitors' Bureau
Box 9480
Amarillo 79105
1-800-692-1338 (Texas); 1-800-654-1902 (outside Texas)

Vast and sparsely populated, the Panhandle region can seem endless and boring to a child, but there are treasures, if you know where to find them. This is legendary country—the land of cowboys, Indians, buffalo, ranchers, outlaws, and oil men. It would be a shame to leave West Texas without introducing the children to the authentic West—rodeos, barbecues, pioneer museums, and plenty of parks and recreation areas.

Summers are hot here, but evenings are nearly always cool with a pleasant breeze; so plan outdoor activities when you can for early morning and early evening. In the middle of a summer day, be sure to use hats, sunscreens, sunglasses, and perhaps carry water if you are going to be exploring in the sun. When driving watch for sudden storms, which can be violent, and flash flood warnings. Of course, the nicest season to visit West Texas is autumn.

Right in the heart of the Panhandle is Amarillo, an old cattle-shipping and railroad town. Once called "Ragtown," it was re-named "Amarillo," Spanish for "Yellow," for the color of a local creek bed. It is a modern city with every convenience, but if you meet a cowboy on the street, he really IS a cowboy.

It was once the largest cattle-shipping point in the world, and the stockyards (which you can visit) are still impressive.

For information about touring a feedlot, call 806-358-3681. To visit the **Livestock Auction,** largest in Texas (100 S. Manhatten, near the Tri-State Fairgrounds), call 806-373-7464. Sales are early in the week; narrated tours are available for groups of 25 or more, but you can visit on your own. Visitors are always welcome at the headquarters of the largest quarter horse registry in the world, the **American Quarter Horse Association** (2701 I-40 East). Except for the statue in front, there isn't a horse on the place, but if you have a kid addicted to horses, it is worth a visit.

A Day in the Old West

Write or call the Convention & Visitors' Bureau ahead of time for information about these packaged day trips. "A Day in the Old West" is one of the packages offered by the Bureau, but you can pick and choose among the activities to create your own schedule. If you choose the package, everything will be taken care of for you, including transportation and meals, at a good price.

Not to be missed is **Cowboy Morning Breakfast** at the famous Figure 3 Ranch (about 45 minutes from Amarillo near

Claude) on the rim of Palo Duro Canyon. You can arrange to be picked up at your motel, or meet at the ranch house (you will get directions when you make reservations), and be carried in horse-drawn wagons to a spectacular site on the rim of the canyon.

There, the hands of the Figure 3 will have prepared on a mesquite fire an old-fashioned ranch breakfast, which is likely to be more than you can eat—meat, eggs, gravy, biscuits, hotcakes, and all the fixins. The grownups will love the campfire coffee.

After breakfast you can explore the beautiful canyon rim area, ride horses, and watch demonstrations of roping, branding, and other cowboy arts. Casual, especially western dress, is appropriate. You'll be back in Amarillo by noon. (Saturday and Sunday mornings and other days when tours are not filled; wagons leave the ranch gates at 8:30 a.m. You definitely need reservations.)

You are on your own for lunch, but the Bureau has supplied a list of restaurants offering special cowboy lunches as part of the package—from western barbecue and beans to rattlesnake meat.

Discovery Center with Harrington Planetarium and the Helium Monument and Museum

Just off I-40 at Nelson
806-355-9547
Hours: Open daily.
Admission free.

The Discovery Center presents excellent exhibits that pique the interest of youngsters. Most are focused on the medical and physical sciences. The ecosphere (an unusual planetarium concept) has various presentations throughout the year. The helium monument is unusual. Even young children will be interested by some of the exhibits, but this will be of most value to school age and older children.

Thompson Park

North Fillmore and 24th Sts
806-378-3000
Hours: Dawn to dusk, daily, year round.
Admission is free (fees for specific activities).

This is one of the nicest city parks we have seen. Its high quality has been maintained over the years, and it is still a good place to spend an afternoon and evening. It is well kept and clean; the attendants are young and cheerful; and it is safe, even after dark.

The park has all the usual amenities: miniature golf, summer theater, tennis courts, swimming pool and places to stroll, fly kites, sail frisbies and picnic.

Storyland Zoo

Hours: 10 till sunset

Located in the park, this is a clean, modern zoo, especially good for small children because of its storybook theme and because so many of the animals are familiar and accessible for petting and feeding.

The best time to visit a zoo is early morning or early evening when the animals are likely to be up and about, eating, fighting, foraging, and taking care of their young. In the heat of the day, the animals are usually asleep in their shelters.

Wonderland

806-373-4712

This is one of the cleanest, safest, and most pleasant city amusement parks that we have seen. It has rides for kids of all ages, from a really tough roller coaster for the teens to a charming little train for the smallest tots. The attendants, many of them local high school and college students, are clean-cut, bright, and cheerful. The rides and the whole area are brightly lit at night, and are a safe place to take the children.

Alibates National Monument

30 miles north on TX 136
806-857-3151 (it is best to call ahead)
Hours: Dawn to dusk, daily, early spring through late fall.
Admission free.

Alibates is a site which has provided flint since before 10,000 B.C. Flint was important to the development of civilization, for it provided a hard, yet workable substance from which to make weapons and tools. There are ruins of ancient, pueblo-like villages and rock art in the area, similar to better-known sites in New Mexico. (These are on private land; ask the Park Service or the Convention and Visitor's Bureau if it is possible to visit.)

The National Park Service conducts daily tours of the monument area from spring through early fall, and the helpful guides are well-informed about the prehistory of this fascinating region and the people and animals, past and present, who have made their homes here.

The tour includes demonstrations of how flint can be worked into useful implements, and its importance to the progress of civilization. In some places, the kids are allowed to gather "samples" to take home.

This can be a fairly hot, rough hike, especially in the heat of the summer, and will be enjoyed most by school-age and older children. Hats, sunscreens, and comfortable walking shoes are a good idea.

Lake Meredith National Recreation Area

P.O. Box 1438
Fritch, Tx 79036
806-857-3151
How to get there: Located north of Amarillo off Hwy 287.

Here you will find fishing, boating, swimming, and picnicking. There is also an abundance of wildlife in this national park area, especially during the winter when many migratory birds are to be seen. This is a natural flyway for Canada geese and other species, many of whom "winter over" in the area. You may see wild geese, Sand Hill Cranes, and many other species of birds, including the roadrunner, as well as many other kinds of small animals which are native to West Texas.

Cal Farley's Boys Ranch

US 385 north of Amarillo
806-372-2341
Admission free.

Established for homeless boys, this is a modern "working ranch" where the kids can see what really composes life on the range. Visitors are always welcome here. Tours begin from the Boys' Center, just inside the gate. If you are on hand for lunch, you will probably be invited to join the residents.

The ranch is built on the site of **Old Tascosa,** an abandoned village whose courthouse has been turned into a museum. There is also a "boot hill" cemetery, with graves of gunfighters. On the way out of Amarillo on I-40, don't miss the famous **Cadillac Garden,** where Stanley Marsh 3 "planted" a row of caddies, of the vintage fin years, noses out of the ground, and called it art. It has since been adorned with graffiti. (The gate is locked, but you get a good view from a rise of ground along the road.)

Balmorhea

Balmorhea State Recreation Area

Four miles west of Balmorhea off Hwy 290 in the Madera Valley
Box 15
Toyahvale 79786
915-375-2370
Admission charged.

During the summer months you can swim in one of the most unusual pools in the country. Part concrete and part natural rock, this is the largest man-made pool in the world. In the center, 30 feet deep, is a spring from which 18 million gallons of water a day flow. Moss grows on the bottom of the pool and tiny fish too quick to catch dart about. Three sizes of inner tubes are for rent from the indoor concession stand which also sells snacks. A tree-shaded picnic area with a playground borders the gigantic pool. Lodging is also available in the park in quaint cabins built during the CCC era of the early thirties. Rates are extremely reasonable.

Lake Balmorhea, three miles southeast of Balmorhea, is kept brimful by the springs and irrigation system, and fishing and boating is available.

Big Bend Country

Big Bend National Park

79834
915-477-2251
Hours: Open year round.
Admission charged.

If you long to get close to nature and far away from civilization, Big Bend National Park is the place to go. Formerly the domain of maurauding Indians and Mexicans, the unpredictable topography lends itself well to losing others and one's self.

It's a long drive to get there, so make sure your car is in peak performance for the trip. Although a spacious lodge

Hiking is a "must" in the gorgeous Big Bend Country whether it's for a day or a month.

Photo by Michael Murphy. Courtesy of Tourism Division, Texas Department of Commerce

provided by the National Park Service will harbor the more timid visitors, it is the vast expanse of land that lures the many campers, hikers, and backpackers to Big Bend.

The two most popular ways to experience Big Bend are by horseback and rafting. South Rim horseback ride that lasts all day and costs $42 per person and a 2½-hour trip that is $17 per person. Call 915-477-2374 to arrange for overnight trips. Rafting is free if you bring your own equipment, but skilled boatman/guides and rigging costs about $35 for a half-day excursion to $75 for an overnight trip.

Park headquarters offers a Hiker's Guide and plenty of free advice on the best way to hike, according to current weather and water conditions. Some marked trails provide an easy path. The **Santa Elena Canyon Nature Trail** is one of the prettiest short walks in the park. The Dagger Flat Interpretive Auto Trail provides an alternate means to view the scenery. Be sure to carry ample water.

There are three campgrounds in Big Bend and park rangers present evening slide programs. Check bulletin boards for information.

Be sure to visit the **Ranger Station.** Rafting permits, which are free, can be obtained at park headquarters.

For reservations at **Chisos Lodge,** call or write National Park Concessions, Inc., Big Bend National Park, TX 79834 (915-477-2291). (See *Camper's Guide to Texas Parks, Lakes, and Forests,* Lone Star Books, Houston, 1986.)

Terlingua

Hwy 170 (Camino del Rio, which begins in Study Butte, runs along the Rio Grande about 140 miles and abruptly ends at Candelaria)
P.O. Box 362
Terlingua 79852
915-371-2234
Lajitas address: Star Route 70, Box 400
Terlingua 79852
915-424-3267

Just outside of Big Bend National Park, you will come to Lajitas, the up-and-coming place on the Big Bend border. Enterprising Walter Mischer of Houston is transforming this sleepy town that has been in existence since the early 1800s into a thriving tourist mecca. But an authentic trading post still reflects the past. The store was built of traditional adobe around the turn-of-the-century to handle business generated by nearby candelilla wax production plants and the good border crossing. Revolutionary Pancho Villa prowled up and down the river in this area, plotting his raids. Bullet holes in the walls attest to the fiery history of the area. The trading post still stocks such things as cowhide strips, wood baskets, and dried chili peppers. Young and old will delight in Clay Henry, the resident beer-drinking goat.

If the row of old-looking houses on the riverside looks like something out of a movie, you are right. Films frequently are shot on this location with real mountains as an impressive backdrop, but the structure actually contains the Badlands Hotel. On the sight where Gen "Blackjack" Pershing housed his troops in the early 1900s is now the Cavalry Post motel. A replica of Ft. Davis officer's quarters has been constructed and now serves as modern condos.

Many amenities are tucked away in this town that vies with neighboring Presidio for the title of hottest spot in the nation. A shaded tram will take you around Lajitas, and geological tours as well as horseback rides in the Badlands where outlaws once lived are offered.

The new **Lajitas Museum** is open year around and boasts a variety of modern displays. There are wildlife dioramas, a desert and cactus garden, and archeological and geological displays.

A float trip down the Rio Grande is an unforgettable experience. You can rent equipment several places in town, and kids absolutely love rafting. There are several river routes to choose from, but the trip down Colorado Canyon is a delight. Several experienced outfitters will make your float trip a really memorable event. Half day trips and overnight trips are available as well as week-long excursions with great riverside cook-outs.

Terlingua was once a ghost town but is gradually being reinhabited. The area post office is here along with several stores and restaurants. Terlingua was a thriving community based on mercury mined here from about 1842 to 1942, when the bottom fell out of the market. All the inhabitants left to find work elsewhere, and Terlingua was auctioned off. In 1984, Bill and Rex Ivey bought the town. The old church, the abandoned school, and Perry's (the original mine owner) mansion are among the structures still standing. Don't allow the kids to scramble around the ruins as they will certainly want to do. Too many abandoned mine shafts could cave in. The Terlingua Ranch has accommodations for visitors by reservation only. Call the Ranch office at 915-371-2416.

Fort Leaton State Historic Site

P.O. Box 1220
Presidio 79845
915-229-3613
How to get there: Four miles southeast of Presidio on FM 170.
Hours: 8 a.m.–4:30 p.m.
Admission free. (Tour fees charged.)

The imposing adobe pueblo-style fortress was built in 1848, just after the Mexican-American War by Benjamin Leaton, early-day soldier-of-fortune and former scalphunter. At his fortress he began to farm the fertile floodplain and engage in trade with the Mexicans and Indians. He soon became a dominant force along the border, almost totally controlling the Indian trade. Leaton was charged with purposely instigating Indian raids into Mexico for livestock that were then bartered at his fortress.

Leaton died after only three years but his widow married again and continued to live at the fortress. Her husband, Edward Hall, used the compound as a freighting center in the sparsely populated area. However, John Burgess, one of Leaton's old buddies, managed to acquire the property from a debt. Hall refused to vacate the premises and was killed. Burgess took over the place and he, too, operated a business there. Burgess was later murdered by one of Leaton's sons, who was also the stepson of Burgess's victim, Edward Hall. The property stood vacant for a number of years but in 1968 it was donated to the state of Texas by Frank Skidmore of El Paso, thus effectively ending the saga of the privately owned fortress. (See *Frontier Forts of Texas,* Lone Star Books, Houston, 1986.)

There is another fortress—or the remains of one—at Shafter on Hwy 67 north of Presidio. The first Anglo-American ranchers constructed protective towers at the corners of their property. Also at Shafter you can visit the site of the old silver mine. Shafter was named after General William Rufus "Pecos Bill" Shafter who reportedly discovered the vein of the precious metal. About $18 million worth of silver was mined here before the mine was closed in the early 1950s.

Canyon

Canyon is often treated like a suburb of Amarillo (which is only half an hour away) and the Amarillo Convention and Visitors' Bureau includes it in its packages, but it is a very nice town in its own right, the home of West Texas State University. We prefer to stay in Canyon when we want to explore the area.

Panhandle-Plains Historical Museum

2401 4th St.
Canyon 79015
806-655-7191
Hours: Open daily, all year.
Admission free.
How to get there: Located on the campus of West Texas State University
in the middle of town.

This is the largest and best among the many museums in this area, a must for the visitor.

Our kids are always interested in Indian lore, and the Hall of the Southern Plains Indians is an excellent introduction to the native Americans who were the "first settlers" of the plains. Through exhibits, collections, and dioramas, the kids can learn what is known about the ancient people who settled in this area, built pueblos, and left artifacts like "rock art," and the theories about what happened to many of these ancient peoples. Then they can learn about daily life among the Plains Indians, how they hunted, what they ate, and how they lived, until the coming of the Europeans.

The Museum tells the "next part" of the story at Pioneer Village which portrays the settlement of the territory by the ranchers and farmers who came here, not so very long ago, to make new lives for themselves and their families. Buildings have been restored and furnished to resemble a turn-of-the-century West Texas town, as though the inhabitants had just stepped out for a few minutes.

The Petroleum Wing contains 75,000 square feet of exhibits about independent oil and gas operators in the Panhandle. There is an excellent collection of transportation devices which tells how the availability of transportation, especially the railroad, "opened up" this country to settlers and commerce. And in the basement is a natural history museum where the children can learn about the native plant and animal life of the region. There is, in fact, more to see here than most children can tolerate in one trip. So you may want to break up your tour.

Palo Duro Canyon State Park

Rt 2 Box 285
Canyon 79015
806-488-2227
Hours: Open all day, all year.
How to get there: Go 12 miles east on TX 217 to Park Rd 5

If your children, like ours, found the Grand Canyon beautiful but remote and inaccessible, they will find Palo Duro a canyon they can see, touch, feel, and hear.

As you drive out toward the Canyon (and you won't know it is there until you reach it), look for the longhorn cattle which are often pastured along the way, descendants of the tough breeds which were the foundation of ranch life.

Stop first at the **Interpretive Center** and **Observation Point,** near the Park entrance, to pick up literature, pay a small fee, get oriented, and use the viewers to look out over the Canyon—children always love viewers.

You are standing along the ragged edge, or escarpment, of the Southern Great Plains, which folks here call the "Caprock." A series of canyons like this, formed by the Brazos River and its tributaries, forms the boundary between the plains (on top of the caprock), which is devoted to agriculture, and the wilder ranchland below.

The scenic drive down into the 15,000 acre park is dramatic (the road is safe); you will drop 1,200 feet and, in terms of archaeological "layers," thousands of years, within a few minutes.

Winding roads lead through the park area, along the creek, with picnic tables and rest facilities scattered here and there. For our children, a day in the canyon meant donning old clothes, packing a picnic lunch, and exploring: climbing the hills, collecting rocks and plant specimens, wading in the streams, and playing "cowboys and Indians," while their parents enjoyed the ever-changing colors on the canyon walls, especially spectacular at sunrise and sunset.

When the children tire of "free play," there are other things to do. A delightful little train, the "Sad Monkey," is a favorite delight. You can also rent horses to explore on. There is a store and concession stand, The Goodnight Trading Post. Facilities for camping are available, but you must make reservations well in advance during the busy season. Be aware that a sudden downpour may cause flash flooding in the canyon.

Not to be missed is the production of Paul Green's historical drama, *Texas*. In the evenings barbecue dinner is served from 6:30 p.m.–8 p.m. near the amphitheatre, before the Pulitzer Prize-winning drama about early Texas Life is presented (8:30 p.m. nightly except Sunday in the summer; call ahead, 806-655-2181, for reservations). The setting under the stars in the Canyon is nearly as impressive as the production, which has a huge cast and is thoroughly professional. You will need a jacket or sweater, for it gets surprisingly cool here at night; a pillow or blanket will make the seating more comfortable.

Goodnight Jeep Tours of the Canyon are available (806-373-7800, or 1-800-692-1338, Texas, or 1-800-654-1902 out of state) and are a terrific way to see the more remote parts of the canyon, outside the park, which you would probably not discover on your own. Twice-daily, four-hour trips leave Amarillo at 8:30 and 1:30, through October. A fee is charged, but is well worth it.

(In case you wonder, "Goodnight," a name you see frequently, is not pure whimsy, but the name of a famous early rancher in the Panhandle.)

Dalhart

XIT Reunion and Rodeo

Chamber of Commerce
P.O. Box 967
Dalhart 79022
Admission free.

Billed as the largest rodeo in the world, the celebration has been held for 50 years, and includes a barbecue, junior rodeo, tractor pull, street parade, pony express races, country/western dance and antique car show. It is held in August, but call for specific dates.

The XIT is one of the most famous old ranches in the region. In the late 1800s it was the largest in the world under barbed wire, and this celebration began as a reunion of hands who had worked on the ranch. The riderless horse which leads the annual parade, and the **Empty Saddle Monument** are tributes to the working cowboy who is so important to the history of the Panhandle. Traditionally, many "old timers" return for the annual celebration, although their ranks are thinning as the years pass. Thousands of visitors as well as natives throng the area during this annual event. (See *The Best of Texas Festivals*, Lone Star Books, Houston, 1986.)

El Paso and Vicinity

Convention and Visitors Bureau
5 Civic Center Plaza
El Paso 79901-1186
915-534-0698
How to get there: Located in the Civic Center downtown.

El Paso is a thriving metropolitan area that holds such diversity as the Sun Bowl, a race track, and a host of Roman Catholic missions, one with a resident ghost.

The Spanish flavor of the city began long ago, before there was a state of Texas and was nourished by the presence of the U.S.-Mexico border that changed as the Rio Grande changed its course. The boundary was stabilized by a concrete waterway in 1963 after a treaty was signed by the two nations. **Chamizal Park,** where the river used to run, is now a buffer zone that was established by the treaty. The land on either side of the border can only be used for recreational/cultural purposes. Both the Mexican and U.S. parks are open to the public. You can enter from San Marcial Street or Delta Drive. A scenic drive in the **Franklin Mountains** affords a birds-eye view of the parks and El Paso.

Just across the border is a great opportunity for the kids to get a taste of life in Mexico. They will surely be impressed by children their size selling gum and such on the street. Shopping is decidedly different—there's definitely the personal touch and haggling is encouraged. A nice shopping center is near the Santa Fe toll bridge. It's best to park on the U.S. side and walk over.

An aerial tramway can give you an eagle-eye view of the Franklin Mountains and beyond. You can catch it at the end of McKinney Avenue, just off Alabama St., and it is open noon–9 p.m. during the summer. Nestled in the mountains is **McKelligon Canyon Amphitheatre** where a lively rendition of history, *Viva El Paso!*, is performed July through August against a backdrop of mountains and stars. For more information call 915-532-2759.

Insights Museum located in the lower level of the Mills Building (303 N. Oregon, 915-542-2990) is a kid-type museum with more than 80 hands-on scientific exhibits about motion, light illusion, space science and human senses. There is a small admission fee with free parking at Park-Rite Garage.

The **El Paso Zoo** is located at Evergreen at Paisano (take exit 23 off I-10 and follow the zoo signs). More than 250 species call this zoo home. California sea lions, spider monkeys and a new South American pavilion featuring a tropical forest and savanna are main attractions. The zoo is open all year and charges admission.

The **Border Patrol Museum** at 310 N. Mesa in the basement of the historic Cortez Building features displays of early day methods as well as current sophisticated surveillance techniques used by the border patrol to preserve the integrity of the U.S. border.

Indian Cliffs Ranch 30 miles east of town (take Fabens exit off I-10 and turn left) offers hayrides, overnight trail rides and picnicking for a fee (915-544-3200).

Southeast of town you will find the tiny community of San Elizario (take Ave. of Americas exit off I-10 to Socorro) that was established as a Spanish town/fort in the late 1700s. The **Socorro Mission** is said to have a ghost that has been captured on film. The original jailhouse is found just past the town square.

Sports enthusiasts will surely delight in seeing first hand where the Christmas Day football game is played in the **Sun Bowl.** Built up against a mountain, the bowl provides free seating for those who care to scale the mountain. And speaking of sun, sunshine is especially bright in this town and so sunglasses are considered a necessity to prevent sunburn to the eyes, even for the young children. Hats help, too.

Tigua Indian Reservation/Living History Pueblo

119 S. Old Pueblo Rd
915-859-7913 or 915-859-3916
Admission charged.
How to get there: Take Avenue of the Americas exit from I-10 East,
*   southeast of El Paso.*

Photo by Richard Reynolds. Courtesy of Tourism Division, Texas Department of Commerce

Kids love the Tigua Indian Reservation and are fascinated with their unique culture still being faithfully preserved. It is an El Paso highlight.

The Tigua Indians still have their niche in America. Their roots go back an impressive 3,100 years, but they arrived in West Texas only yesterday, so to speak, in 1540 after being rousted out of New Mexico. The survival skills of the tribe have served them well here, and they now are nurturing their 600 members into a cohesive group. The focal point of the tribe's economy is the multi-million dollar pueblo where their culture is shared with visitors.

Influenced by early-day missionaries, the Tigua Indians became predominantly Christian but their present-day culture reflects a blending of their traditional heritage with their new beliefs. Native dances, celebrating various aspects of nature are performed daily during the summer in a pueblo's kiva, and the round room that was the center for religious festivities and ceremonies.

The Tiguas are now famous for their tender, tasty fajitas and hot chili served in the restaurant in the pueblo. Reservations are recommended for this popular establishment. After lunch, you can enter the inner part of the pueblo for a taste of Tigua life. A row of bee-hive shaped ovens line one path, and the Tiguas bake bread daily in these ovens. The delectable round loaves are sold in the gift shop. Although the ingredients have been modernized, the bread is essentially the same as it was hundreds of years ago and will literally provide kids with a taste of yesteryear.

A tour of the pueblo rooms will reveal Tiguas quietly creating meticulous and beautiful pottery that you can buy. Designs that decorate the pottery are painted by hand without a pattern and thus reflect the mood of the artist.

Kids love the Tigua Reservation and are fascinated with their unique culture that is being preserved. It is an El Paso highlight for visitors.

Fort Bliss

El Paso
915-568-2121
Admission free.
How to get there: Enter base off Airport Road behind El Paso
 International Airport, through Robert E. Lee gate.

Originally established during the Mexican-American War in 1846 as a strategically important post to protect the United States, Fort Bliss has expanded its horizons considerably. Today, Fort Bliss is the world's largest NATO air defense center in the world. The early day mission was also to protect travelers, pioneers, and settlers from Comanche, Kiowa, and Apache Indians. Ft. Bliss, along with all other federal posts in Texas became Confederate property when Texas seceded from the Union. U.S. troops arrived again in 1865 but departed in 1877. Without federal troops, lawlessness flourished in the area and concerned citizens united and managed to get the fort reopened. Since that time, the fort commanders have pursued Pancho Villa, trained over 60 thousand soldiers for World War II, seen the last U.S. Cavalry dismounted in favor of motor driven equipment, and trained anti-aircraft artillery specialists.

The present NATO base has 20,000 troops and trains fighting men from more than 25 countries with special areas designated for use by each country. Fort Bliss has several museums that are open to the public free of charge. One is a replica of the original fort (Bldg. 600) (915-568-5412).

Fort Bliss in El Paso is the largest NATO air defense center in the world and offers little soldiers a close-up look at huge tanks, anti-aircraft guns, and missiles.

The **Air Defense Artillery Museum** (Bldg. 5000) has a vast array of military guns and equipment from different war eras. Outside on the grounds, the kids and grown-ups can explore huge battle tanks, anti-aircraft guns, and missiles. You are free to wander around in the area, and there are no restrictions on picture taking. The **Cavalry Museum** (Bldg. 2407) chronicles the history of the 3rd Armored Cavalry Regiment that is still stationed at Ft. Bliss. This regiment provided the United States with over 50 generals (915-568-4518).

More than 20 of the original buildings of the fort, erected in 1893, are still in use.

Hueco Tanks State Historical Park

Rural Rt 3 Box 1
El Paso 79935
915-857-1135
Hours: 8 a.m.–dusk, summers.
Admission charged.
How to get there: Located 33 miles east of El Paso off US 62/180 on
*   FM 2775.*

During your drive to Hueco Tanks, you will pass through the ancient **salt flats** that provided salt to early settlers. Although no usable salt remains, miles and miles of white will stretch before you. You will finally reach an 860-acre, 300-foot high rock pile in the middle of nowhere. Hueco Tanks is an impressive sight. Formed 34 million years ago, the volcanic mass contains shallow depressions called huecos (the Spanish word for hollows) that were formed as the molten lava flowed underground. Later erosion of the lighter elements left an awe-inspiring outcropping that has attracted visitors since Folsom man 10,000 years ago. Depressions in the rock collect water that was a precious commodity to the people who traveled through here.

As various Indian tribes came to camp at the rocks, they left their mark by painting figures that tell of significant events in their lives. Distinct cultures are represented by thousands of paintings dating from approximately 6,000 years ago.

Picnic areas and playgrounds are located in a shady area, but this park can get intensely hot. Also on the grounds of the park is the ruins of the Butterfield Overland Stagecoach stop.

Carlsbad Caverns

Carlsbad Chamber of Commerce/Visitors Bureau
P.O. Box 910
Carlsbad, NM 88220
505-887-6516—Visitors' Center, 505-785-2232
Hours: 7 a.m.–8 p.m., summer; 8–5:30, winter. Last elevator down
*   two hours before closing, last walk-in three and a half hours before*
*   closing.*
Admission charged.

When you are this far west, you won't want to miss crossing the state line and visiting the spectacular Carlsbad Caverns. The evening bat flight is just one of the many sights visitors enjoy.

You'll be glad to know the bats hole up in only one area of the multi-section cave and stay put until sunset, after the cavern is closed for the night. The bats are in residence usually from May to December.

The caves themselves are part of the great underground portion of a huge mountain ridge that circles the Permian Basin. El Capitan, the great outcropping in Guadalupe National Park is part of that ridge but was uplifted by massive earth movements eons ago. The caverns developed from water that entered fractures and slowly dissolved the limestone reef and the process is still going on today.

The main chambers of the cave are at three levels—200, 750, and 830 feet below the surface of the earth. The magnificent cavernous rooms have been endowed with fanciful names, such as the King's Chamber and the Queen's Chamber. The largest room is more than 14 acres big, with a 200-foot ceiling. Paths through the caverns are sometimes slippery and steep, so non-skid shoes are needed for everyone. You might want a light wrap. Acoustic phones are available for rent in the spacious visitors' center that also has a nursery for the little ones. The complete walk-in tour takes about three and a half hours, but shorter versions are available and an elevator out can provide relief from the hike.

Nearby **White's City,** designed for Cavern tourists, has restaurants and a museum that features a 6,000 year old mummy as well as a doll collection.

Guadalupe Mountains National Park

3225 National Parks Hwy
Carlsbad, NM 88220
915-828-3251
Hours: 7 a.m.–6 p.m., daily, June–Aug.; 8 a.m.– 4:30 p.m.,
*   Sept.–May.*
Admission charged for camping.
How to get there: Located on US Hwy 62/180, 55 miles southwest of
*   Carlsbad, NM and 110 miles east of El Paso, TX.*

Once privately owned, the highest peak in Texas and its adjacent thousand-foot cliff, El Capitan, are now open to anyone industrious enough to climb to the top. A number of trails are marked in the park, from brief half-hour excursions to the four hour hike to the top of the 8,751-foot-high Guadalupe peak. Even young children can experience a short mountain climb or a walk through a level canyon. Be sure to check in with park headquarters before you begin. You must carry along a good supply of water, and good hiking boots are recommended for mountain climbing.

There are two campgrounds on either side of the park, and park rangers present a program at dark around a campfire during the summer.

El Capitan in the Guadalupe Mountains east of El Paso is the highest peak in Texas.

McKittrick Canyon has a reputation as one of the most beautiful natural retreats in the state. Once the hideout of outlaw Kid McKittrick in the 1800s the canyon is now deserted. The Kid was a bank robber who would flee into the canyon and vanish from pursuing posses. He was never caught there, and old timers report that his cache of loot is still hidden in the caves that dot Guadalupe mountains.

The Guadalupe Mountains were once deep under water and were formed by millions of tiny organisms that secret-ed lime. Then, by nature's awesome force, the reef was partly thrust up. El Capitan heralds the end of the exposed mountain reefs. Carlsbad Caverns is part of that same system which has been eroded and decorated by water seepage. El Capitan was a natural landmark for early travelers across America. You might want to hike over to the ruins of **Pine Springs Station,** one mile west of the visitors' center or the stagestop for the Butterfield stagecoach station built in 1858.

Fort Davis

Fort Davis National Historic Site

P.O. Box 1456
915-426-3224
Fort Davis 79734
*Hours: 8 a.m.–5 p.m., Sept.–May, and from 8 a.m.–6 p.m., summers.
  Closed Dec. 25 and Jan. 1.*
Admission charged.
How to get there: Located on the northern edge of Ft. Davis TX.

Fort Davis makes an excellent centerpoint for travel around the Davis Mountain area. Traveling 30 miles can reveal such wonders as deer and antelope grazing in open fields, the lofty McDonald Observatory complex, the **Chihuahuan Desert Museum,** a dude ranch and, or course, the fort itself. Fort Davis is a partially preserved fort that was strategically located in the Davis mountains. One of the string of forts across Texas, it afforded protection to settlers, traders, and gold miners in the late 1800s when Indians still

At historic Fort Davis, bugle calls resound throughout the day from reveille to a school call for children living on the post.

roamed the area. The fort headquarters now houses a small museum/interpretive center. The main officers' quarters boast elaborately furnished rooms such as a parlor and dining, and music room.

Bugle calls are given throughout the day to recall such events as reveille, sick call, and school call for the children who lived on the post. A slide presentation further explains life during the bloody Indian-Cavalry days. Upon Texas' secession from the Union in 1861, Fort Davis was closed. The post was subsequently occupied by Confederate soldiers, who launched a futile campaign to conquer New Mexico. Then, Apaches attacked the fort and largely destroyed it. The fort was later reconstructed and in 1867, after the war, federal troops returned. It was from Fort Davis that Buffalo Soldiers, composed of many newly freed blacks, gallantly campaigned against Geronimo until his surrender in 1886, thus ending the Apache wars.

Fort Davis State Park

P.O. Box 786
Ft. Davis 79734
915-426-3337
Hours: Office is open 8 a.m.–5 p.m.

Four miles northwest of town on Hwy 118 is a well-equipped camping and picnicking area complete with playground. Indian Lodge, a delightful pueblo-style hotel, offers inexpensive lodging within the park.

Prude Ranch, once just a working ranch now is also a dude ranch with unique accommodations. There are trailer hook-ups, a beautiful lodge with hot tubs, lighted tennis courts, and trail rides. (P.O. Box 1431, Fort Davis, 79734 (915-426-3202).)

The University of Texas Observatory at Mount Locke

W. L. Moody Visitors' Information Center
915-426-3263
Hours: Visitors' Center open 9 a.m.–5 p.m., Sun.; closed Thanksgiving, Christmas, and New Year's Day.
Admission free.
How to get there: Mount Locke is 13 miles north of Ft. Davis State Park on Hwy 118.

The drive up Mount Locke, the highest peak in the Davis Mountains at 6,800 feet is spectacular, but the summit reveals further wonders—two gigantic telescopes and several smaller ones perched on the tip top of the mountain. Guided tours are conducted at the astronomy complex each afternoon at 2:00 and June–August at 9:30 a.m. to explain the workings of the huge eye that gathers light and by means of sophisticated computers, translates it into information that helps men get to the moon and spacecrafts to circle Jupiter.

Star gazing is offered every Tuesday and Saturday evening at sunset, clouds permitting, through research quality telescopes with good views of galaxies, planets and other celestial objects. It gets cool on desert nights, so dress warmly and bring binoculars if you can. You never know what will appear in the clear Texas air.

A Visitors' Center is at the base of the mountain.

Fort Stockton

Chamber of Commerce
P.O. Box C
Fort Stockton 79735
915-336-2264

Beginning with the huge 20-foot-long, 18-foot-high statue of **Paisano (Roadrunner) Pete,** Ft. Stockton offers visitors a variety of accessible and interesting sights. The town has 16 state historic medallion sites provided along a well-marked route that takes you to the oldest house in Ft. Stockton (1859) and the **Guard House** on the old fort grounds which still contains prisoners' chains in the dungeon. The early-day importance of Fort Stockton is reflected by the **zero stone** located next to the courthouse. All surveys of the surrounding area were based on the location of this stone.

Fort Stockton was built near the seven springs that compose the Comanche Springs system. One major spring once flowed 60 million gallons of water a day. However, an extensive modern irrigation system tapping the underground aquifer caused the springs to stop flowing several years ago and left the town almost high and dry. Experts predict the springs will flow again about 1990, and indeed they have begun to gurgle. The town stages a gala Water Carnival the third week-end in July at the beautiful **Comanche Springs Pavilion** and Swimming Pool. Otherwise, you may find a refreshing dip a welcome respite from the dry desert air.

The family-owned **Warnock Dairy,** located on Hwy 18 just out of town, in keeping with the accommodating spirit of the town, was built to provide easy viewing of the dairy process. Children are welcome to watch as cows are milked (twice a day) while taped music is played to keep the cows contented. Glass pipes were specially installed to show the milk flowing from the cows into the processing room where it is pasteurized, homogenized, and then bottled. An assortment of cows mill around in the corrals just outside the dairy.

On Hwy 67, twenty-one miles east of town, you can ponder awesome **dinosaur tracks** preserved in the limestone of a creek bed.

Also a well-preserved stagecoach stop of the **Overland/ Butterfield Stage Line** is located 20 miles east of town on I-10 at a modern rest stop. There you can stretch your legs just as stagecoach riders did likewise a hundred years ago.

A gleeful Paisano Pete, the world's largest roadrunner, greets visitors to Fort Stockton.

The kitchen of the Annie Riggs Hotel is one of the many rooms open to visitors in this museum dedicated to the woman who ran what was surely the best hotel in the West.

Annie Riggs Museum

301 S. Main St.
Fort Stockton 79735
915-336-2167
Hours: 10 a.m.–8 p.m., Mon.–Sat., 1:30 p.m.–8 p.m., Sun.,
*   summers. 10 a.m.–5 p.m., Mon.–Sat., 1:30 p.m.–5 p.m., Sun.,*
*   Sept.–May.*
Admission charged.

The Annie Riggs Museum is dedicated to the woman who ran what was surely the best hotel in the West. It's easy to envision cowboys, ranchers and entrepreneurs sitting around the porch that circles the hotel or inside in the courtyard. You can enter most of the rooms that now hold such excellent exhibits as a 21,000-year-old mammoth's tooth found in the area and a curling iron ready to be heated in the chimney of a kerosene lamp. The kitchen has an icebox, a stove that once heated the waffle iron for hotel guests' breakfasts, and an old turn-the-knob/turn-the-bottles Coke machine that can still provide a cold drink. (See *A Guide to Historic Texas Inns and Hotels/2nd Edition*, Lone Star Books, Houston, 1985.)

Lubbock

Chamber of Commerce
P.O. Box 561
Lubbock 79408

Lubbock is a young, bold city, the home of Texas Tech University and two other colleges, high-tech industry, modern agriculture, and a medical center. Named for a civil war colonel from Georgia who settled here, the city is also known as the hometown of Buddy Holly and the Crickets, whose music (and name) inspired the Beatles. **Buddy Holly Park,** at the Civic Center, has a statue of the entertainer.

One of Lubbock's charms is an abundance of small, accessible city parks, many of them built around the "playa" lakes which abound on the High Plains (and, long ago, were used as Buffalo wallows) and are the source for replenishment of the Ogallala Aquifer, the reservoir of underground water upon which agriculture here depends.

In these parks, one finds resident ducks and, in season, wildfowl who often "winter over" here rather than continuing south to Mexico. Bird lovers are often surprised by the number and variety of wild birds in this region.

One of our favorite local parks is **Maxey Park** (Quaker, just south of 19th Street) but the largest and most popular is MacKenzie Park.

MacKenzie Park

Broadway, East of Downtown
806-762-6411 (City Parks and Recreation Department)
Hours: Dawn till dark, daily, year round.
Admission free, but concessions have fees.

MacKenzie is a huge park with all the usual amenities: golf, tennis, picnicking, and places to stroll, fly kites, and enjoy the outdoors. There is a small amusement park, Joyland, open in the evening. The Canyon Lakes District, adjacent to the park, has been upgraded and improved greatly in recent years, and has lakes, waterfalls and picnic areas.

A "must" for visitors is **Prairie Dog Town,** a concrete enclosure which contains (more or less—they keep moving out into adjacent areas) these cute, fat little rodents who are native to the region.

Out on the plains, prairie dogs (a smaller cousin of Eastern groundhogs or woodchucks) are a problem to farmers and ranchers, for their burrows create holes which snare horses, cows, and people. But here in the park, the prairie dogs lead a charmed life, and all they have to do is entertain visitors with their antics.

Often you will see brown bunnies and owls in the enclosure as well: they seem to co-exist peacefully. Further afield in the park you will find jackrabbits, three times the size of their eastern cousins, road-runners, and various kinds of birds.

The Museum of Texas Tech University with Moody Planetarium/ The Ranching and Heritage Center

4th Street and Indiana Avenue
Box 4349
Lubbock 79409
806-742-1498
Hours: 9 a.m.–4:30 p.m., Mon.–Sat., 1 p.m.–4:30 p.m., Sun.
Free admission.

Lubbock people are justly proud of this excellent museum, which has a fine collection of permanent and rotat-

The Museum of Texas Tech University and the Moody Planetarium offer a range of sights from Western art to artifacts from the nearby Lubbock Lake Site.

You can't go to Lubbock without a visit to the Ranching Heritage Center where you can trace the history of ranching on the High Plains of Texas.

ing exhibits focusing mostly on Western art and cultural objects, but including other art collections as well. There are artifacts from the Lubbock Lake Site archaeological dig, and information about the pre-history of this fascinating region. Kids are always fascinated by dinosaurs.

Shows at the planetarium vary with the season and are frequently changed, but they are always geared toward children.

Adjacent to the museum is the **Ranching Heritage Center,** committed to preserving the ranching heritage which is so important to the people of West Texas. The outdoor exhibit recreates pioneer days with 30 historical structures that have been moved here from various places in the re-

gion, restored, and furnished authentically in keeping with the time they were lived in.

The entire outdoor area is protected from nearby highways and modern buildings by earthen embankments or berms, so that you have a sense of having stepped back into history—especially in the summer when guides in native dress are on duty to explain the exhibits, demonstrate crafts, and answer questions.

Children will be fascinated by the "dugout," the first home of the pioneer family. Keep track of the progress of the family as it grew more prosperous, through the various kinds of homes that are presented, keeping in mind that lumber for building them often had to be brought great distances by cart or, later, the railroad. Little natural timber grows on the high plains.

Finally, there is a splendid Victorian mansion where the well-to-do rancher lived. There is also a one-room schoolhouse, blacksmith shop, milk and meat houses, bunkhouse, and the ranch headquarters, including outhouses and other "necessary" buildings.

In the main building exhibits tell the story of the history of ranching with such artifacts as wagons, saddles, branding irons, and Western art and bronzes. Very often there are guides in pioneer dress to explain the exhibits and demonstrate such arts as making lye soap, cooking sourdough bread, and shoeing horses. (See *Historic Homes of Texas*, Lone Star Books, Houston, 1987.)

Lubbock Lake Site

Loop 289 and Clovis
806-742-2442
Hours: Tours given Sat. mornings, June–July and at other times by
  arrangement.
Admission free.
How to get there: Located two miles north of Texas Tech University.

This is one of the most famous archaeological "digs" in the world, to which people come from as far away as China. Many remarkable artifacts have been uncovered here. The site is most likely to interest the young anthropologist or archaeologist, especially in the summer when there is more activity. On the other hand, you can visit and find nothing but an open hole, so call ahead to see what is happening and get directions before going. Artifacts from the site are on display at the museum.

Llano Estacado Winery

FM 1585
Lubbock
806-745-2258
Hours: Tours at noon–6 p.m., Sat. and 1 p.m.–6 p.m., Sun.
Admission free.

Hardly anyone expects to find vineyards in West Texas, but in fact this is one of the fastest-growing industries in the area and local wines are receiving national attention. Our children were quite fascinated to see how wines are made.

Marfa/Alpine

Marfa Chamber of Commerce
Main Street across from the Courthouse
Marfa 79843
915-729-4942

The mysterious twinkling lights in the sky known as the Marfa Lights are the main attraction of the little town of Marfa. The fickle and flickering lights have been seen since at least 1883 when a rancher noticed strange lights in the distance and feared they were Apache signal fires. Later searching the countryside, he found nothing. Since then, many other sightings have occurred, so much so that the Texas Highway Department has paved a viewing area nine miles out of Marfa where the sightings usually occur.

Everyone from occultist to UFO buffs have proffered an explanation. One computer operator returning home late one evening reported he saw a cantaloupe-size red ball of light speeding toward him. He frantically tried to drive away but the ball of light remained with him for two miles before it suddenly disappeared. The answer, which will calm many a fevered brow, is an atmospheric phenomena exactly opposite of the familiar mirage that appears in the desert and on roads. The high elevation and topographical location of the site of the lights creates a fairly well defined boundary between the heat radiating from the ground and the cool mountain air. When rays of distant lights hit this boundary, they are bent back to earth. The lights far from the observer such as car lights, bright planets, and stars can be the light source.

Marfa's surprisingly cool climate affords summer vacation a pleasant retreat from blistering heat and the kids should enjoy drinking their excellent water. The historic **Paisano Hotel** (next to the Chamber of Commerce) proudly displays autographed pictures of Elizabeth Taylor, James Dean, and other stars of the movie *Giant* that was filmed

Nestled in the heart of the Davis Mountains is Marfa, famous for its mysterious Marfa ghost lights and fine old buildings such as the Paisano Hotel.

outside of town. The grand and ornate hotel was built in anticipation of an oil boom that never materialized in Marfa.

The stately Presidio county courthouse, built in 1886 will allow you to climb to the dome for a beautiful view of the Davis Mountains.

Alpine Chamber of Commerce
106 North 3rd
Alpine 79830
915-837-2326

Alpine, so named for the surrounding "Alps," also provides a relatively cool haven. Designated as the safest city in the U.S., according to recent studies, Alpine is a gateway to the vast area known as Big Bend.

Museum of the Big Bend

Sul Ross University Campus
915-837-8143
Hours: 9 a.m.–5 p.m., Tues.–Sat., 1 p.m.–5 p.m., Sun. Closed Mon. Admission free.

Various horsedrawn vehicles, including a bullet-riddled stagecoach are contained in this museum. Kids can also ponder the original "big wheel," an early 1900s bicycle. There is also a pioneer-day general store that has been reconstructed so well that you can almost feel you are entering to buy a sack of beans.

At the **Sul Ross Range Animal Science Center** on Hwy 67/90 east of town, the kids can see where butchers and horseshoers learn their trade. Students here also study range grasses and are taught the proper way to break a horse. Some animals are on the site and admission is free.

Midland

Midland Convention and Visitors' Bureau

P.O. Box 1890
Midland 79702
915-683-3381

Midland is situated in the middle of the Permian Basin oil field that covers some 100,000 square miles of rich oil strata. Street names such as Shell, Gulf, and Humble reflect the importance of oil to this town that began as a cattle center.

Haley Memorial Library

1805 Indiana
Midland 79702
Hours: 9 a.m.–noon, 1 p.m.–5 p.m., Mon.–Fri. Closed Sat. and Sun.
Admission free.
How to get there: Located in downtown Midland.

This library, built by J. Evetts Haley, dean of Texas historians, and dedicated to his first wife, is proof that cattle ranching days are not forgotten. It houses the world's best collection of information on the history of the Southwest. Some of the books written by Mr. Haley are on sale at the library and he will autograph them himself when he's in town.

The gem of the library is the original mission bell from the Alamo, personally acquired by Haley in 1974. A number of western art bronzes are also on display.

Permian Basin Petroleum Museum, Library, and Hall of Fame

1500 Interstate 20 West
Midland 79701
915-683-4403
Hours: 9 a.m.–5 p.m., Mon.–Sat., 2 p.m.–5 p.m., Sun.
Admission charged. Strollers available.

It is Texas's number one industry, wars are fought over it, and it has been the blessing and/or doom for thousands of people. Small wonder, the Permian Basin Petroleum Museum was opened to glorify and explain the elusive underground natural resource—oil. The museum covers not only the history of oil from its formation in the Permian Sea 500 million years ago but also modern-day complex production techniques.

Antique drilling rigs and fascinating displays are just a small part of the excellent Permian Basin Petroleum Museum in Midland.

Wind through the labyrinth of rooms and you will discover yourself in a 1920s boomtown, face to face with a tool dresser on a real drilling platform. You can witness an oil well blow out and walk through a 250,000-year-old sea that explains how decaying shellfish not only provided the substance for oil but the rock it is buried in. A favorite room for the kids is where a mock nitroglycerine detonation illustrates how shock waves were once used to loosen oil from the rock. Push the button and you're in for a surprise! The process of finding the oil, acquiring the mineral rights, drilling and production are depicted in this fine petroleum museum.

An outdoor display on the museum ground displays oil patch equipment. All of the rigs are the cable-tool type, invented by the Chinese before 600 B.C. and still used today. Two "stripper pump jacks" methodically dip up and down on the museum's front lawn.

Monahans

Monahans Sandhills State Park

Box 1738
Monahans 79756
915-943-2092
Admission charged.
How to get there: Located 6 miles NE of Monahans, off I-20, on Park Road 41.

These unique sand dunes, some 90 feet tall, are believed to be from the Trinity sandstone formation, and collected by the Permian Sea which once covered this area. There are evidences of human occupation from as far back as 12,000 years ago. The Indians camped here temporarily, finding game, abundant fresh water beneath the sands, and native acorns and mesquite beans which they ground and used for food.

Spanish explorers more than 400 years ago were the first Europeans to report these vast hills of sand, part of a dune field that extends about 200 miles, from south of Monahans west and north into New Mexico.

There are only a few areas of the country were your family can visit a dune field and learn about the forces which shaped it. Although most of the dunes have been stabilized by vegetation growing on them, inside the park area there are still several "on the move," active dunes which ebb and flow and change shape in response to the prevailing winds.

Stop first at the **Sandhills Interpretive Center,** where you can get information and brochures and where your questions about the dunes will be answered by helpful attendants. The Center has large one-way glass windows, where you can watch wildlife come to the feeding stations just outside (the best time is early morning and early evening).

Armed with your guidebook, follow a self-guided nature trail which winds in and out among the dunes.

On weekends during the summer, visitors can attend campfire programs, presented by park personnel, on natural history, Indian lore, and other outdoor topics.

At the concession stand, an old railroad section house, the kids will want to rent boards and disks and try "sand-surfing," sliding down the dunes, which is great fun. There are also trailer sites and picnic spots and many families like to camp here.

Million Barrel Museum

400 East Fourth St.
Monahans 79756
915-943-8401

This new outdoor museum, still in the process of development, focuses on the railroad which opened this country to settlement in 1881. Agriculture, ranching and the oil industry are presented. The Million Barrel Oil Tank, built in 1928 and soon abandoned, is the nucleus of the museum.

Photo courtesy of Tourism Division, Texas Department of Commerce

For a gigantic sandpile, don't miss Monahans Sandhills State Park. Pails and shovels welcome.

Odessa

Odessa Convention and Visitors' Bureau
P.O. Box 3626
Odessa 79760
915-322-8189

Globe Theatre of the Great Southwest

2308 Shakespeare Road
Odessa 79761
Hours: 9 a.m.–5 p.m.
Admission free.

Odessa is the oil field's hard hat town named after a city in Russia. Ironically, the town's main attraction is the epitome of esoteric culture—an exact replica of Shakespeare's own theater in London. You'll want to show your kids this culmination of a high school student's idea. An English literature student brought a model of the Globe to class and commented that it would be exciting to have a life-size replica of the master bard's theater in Odessa. (See *Amazing Texas Monuments and Museums*, Lone Star Books, Houston, 1984.)

Odessa Meteor Crater

Hours: Open year round.
Admission free.
How to get there: Take US Hwy 80 West.

Here you can see where a gigantic meteorite fall sprinkled the area and left a deep indention, now largely filled with silt. A caretaker still digs for meteor fragments, finding them three to four feet down, and he will be happy to sell one to you.

Pecos

West of the Pecos Museum

120 East First Street
Pecos 79772
915-445-2406 (Chamber of Commerce)
Hours: 9 a.m.–6 p.m., Mon.–Sat., 2 p.m.–6 p.m., Sun. Closed Mon.
Admission charged.

A quick jaunt off I-20 will take you to Pecos, once the home of gunfighters, now home of the world-famous Pecos cantaloupe. If the term "west of the Pecos" means nothing to you now, it certainly would have a hundred or so years ago, for the Pecos river was sort of a boundary, with the fearsome Indians and outlaws on one side and settlers on the other. The West of the Pecos Museum is housed in the restored **Orient Hotel** that was the site of several "street justice" killings. The museum contains pioneer items and even an Indian mummy.

The old west is further depicted in a two block downtown area, complete with a replica of **Judge Roy Bean's saloon** that served as his court of justice in Langtry, Texas.

Old Pecos Town also boasts the grave and wooden headstone of the notorious gunfighter Clay Allison, known as the "Gentleman Gunfighter." Allison died an inglorious death by falling off a freight wagon while he was drunk. It seems the townsfolk wanted to keep their distance from him in death as in life, for he has a whole cemetery to himself.

A rip-roaring rodeo is held in Pecos every July Fourth weekend. Pecos claims to have put on the first official rodeo where cowboys from surrounding areas competed for superiority.

Pecos also has a mini-zoo in its **Municipal Park** that borders I-20 south of town. There's plenty of room for the kids to roam near to the deer, antelope, and buffalo residing in the zoo.

San Angelo

Convention and Visitors' Bureau
500 Rio Concho Drive
915-653-1206 or 915-655-4136
Hours: 8:30 a.m.–5 p.m., Mon.–Fri.

When you arrive in San Angelo, signs will guide you to the modern visitors' center where you can reap a good supply of information on this river city. In addition to the Concho river that winds 12 miles through the city, the town is also embraced by three large lakes, **Nasworthy, Twin Buttes,** and **O. C. Fisher,** all offering good fishing.

A walking tour, as well as a driving tour, provides a taste of the early days of San Angelo. The site of the **Elkhorn Wagon Yard** is marked. This is where emigrants on their way west and families and ranchers from the surrounding area camped while picking up supplies in town. Those early-day shopping commuters could not afford the luxury of a hotel room, so they stayed in this version of a "KOA" park.

Kids will enjoy **Donaho's Saddle Shop** located on historic Concho Street. It opened for business in 1890 and one of its customers was the infamous Pancho Villa. Rector Storey is now the proprietor/saddlemaker and will be glad to explain the three-year apprenticeship necessary to become a saddlemaker and the nationwide demand for the saddles, which cost about $1,000 each.

Mom and Dad will have a few laughs at the **Bordello Museum,** still located at the original site at 18 E. Concho. Mrs. Evelyn Hill who owns the antique store below, has spruced up the original furnishings that were found intact in 1976; however, the brothel was closed by Texas Rangers in 1946.

For the price of a fishing license (not necessary for children under 17) kids can try their hand at catching a mussel in the **Concho River** that might reveal a lovely lavender pearl. The rare native Texas gems are sold at stores in town.

A fully-equipped hometown amusement park is nestled among trees by the side of the river. **Neff's Amusement Park** opens when the weather turns warm in the spring and closes when it turns cold in the winter. Hours are 6 p.m. to 10 p.m. (915-653-3014).

INDEX

———————————☆———————————

M

N

DATE DUE
